PRAYING BODY AND SOUL

Praying Body and Soul
METHODS AND PRACTICES OF
ANTHONY DE MELLO

Adapted and enlarged by
Gabriel Galache SJ

the columba press

First published in 1997 by
the columba press
55A Spruce Avenue, Stillorgan Industrial Park,
Blackrock, Co Dublin

This edition 2004
Originally published in Portuguese as *Corpo e Alma em Oração*
by Edições Loyola, São Paulo, Brazil

Cover by Bill Bolger
Origination by The Columba Press
Printed in Ireland by ColourBooks Ltd, Dublin

ISBN 1 85607 195 2

AN/248.3

Table of Contents

A Note to the reader

'Do you want to be happy?' is a famous question Father Anthony de Mello SJ used to ask at retreats. He would go on to show that we already were happy, that happiness was our natural way of being. Why is it that often we don't experience this happiness? Because we concentrate on what we don't have, even though we have all that we need to be happy.

So what can we do?

Anthony de Mello suggests that we can always learn to experience our happiness. We can learn to wake up, to let go, and to let God. We can start to give prayer its place in our lives.

This book offers an intimate retreat with Anthony de Mello, who was a master-teacher of both the Eastern ways of meditation and the Western traditions of prayer, especially the Ignatian Exercises. Little step by little step, he leads us into the life-changing practices of prayer – prayer that includes the body, the mind, and the soul, our own experiences, the experience of the people of God as reflected in the holy scriptures, and the teachings of the church.

To join de Mello doesn't require any previous knowledge or experience in prayer, and neither does previous knowledge take away from the journey offered here. The book can be used for a retreat or as a guide to daily meditation. It serves as well in a group setting as with individuals. You can read it in silence or out loud. And you can expect to refer back to de Mello's lessons over and over again, as he has left us a gift for a lifetime.

Enjoy it!

– *The Publisher*

1

EXERCISE

Bodily Sensations

Begin this prayer hour with the relaxation and silence exercise below. Remember that *feeling* is not *thinking*:

1. Take up a comfortable and relaxing position. Your eyes may be gently closed or fixed on some object nearby, more or less three feet away.
2. Feel your clothes touching your shoulders.
3. Feel your back gently against the chair.
4. Feel your neck, gently moving your head forward and back, right and left.
5. Feel your chest expanding as you inhale, and relaxing as you exhale.
6. Become aware of the feelings on your right arm … in your left arm … in your right hand and in your left hand. Keep your hands open, in a receptive and relaxed manner on your legs. Also feel your hands, lightly moving each finger.
7. Feel the soles of your feet touching your shoes.

FOCUS

• Simply getting in contact with oneself and feeling the reactions of the body are helpful for entering into dialogue with God, but the greatest obstacle to interior silence is nervous tension.

• Eight or ten minutes of exercises at the beginning of prayer will be enough to feel relaxed and at peace, and to find in silence a climate suitable for contemplation. If we should meet God during the relaxation exercises, we can extend the time devoted to those exercises without fear.

• Sitting straight up in a chair is helpful.

CONTEMPLATION

God's Plan

1. God's saving plan in Jesus Christ (Eph 1:3-14): This text shows God's saving plan in Christ Jesus. It expresses overflowing praise celebrating the spread of God's blessing: 'Blessed be the God and Father of our Lord Jesus Christ, who has blessed us in Christ with every spiritual blessing in the heavenly places' (Verse 3). God is further praised for all his graces in Christ, also in verses 6, 12, and 14. God's Plan is achieved:

- in our selection (verses 4-5): God has chosen us to be holy;
- in being children (5): God has made us all adoptive children;
- in liberation (6-7): by his blood we are liberated;
- in kinship (8-10): we have been united in Christ;
- in inheritance (11-12): we have been made to share in God's glory;
- in the gift of the Holy Spirit (13-14): we are marked with the sign of the Spirit.

2. God's particular plan (Jer 1:5): In this text we find God's particular plan for a specific person, Jeremiah. We may take it that God says to each one of us the same words spoken to Jeremiah: 'Before I formed you in the womb I knew you, and before you were born I consecrated you; I appointed you a prophet to the nations.'

3. God's presence in the life of human beings (Ps 138, 139): In psalm 138, the psalmist expresses his wonder as he experiences

- God's intimate presence in his life (verses 1-6);
- the universal presence (7-12);
- God's loving presence (13-18).

> *One day Saint Thérèse of Jesus,*
> *in a moment of closeness to Jesus,*
> *introduced herself by saying:*
> *'I am Thérèse of Jesus,'*
> *and Jesus came back with these words:*
> *'I am Jesus of Thérèse.'*

2

EXERCISE

Breathing Sensations

1. Feel the air passing through your nose as you breathe. Feel the air and how it is: warm air? cool air?
2. Feel the areas where you feel it. Inhale the air through your nose slowly in order to feel it.
3. Feel whether more air comes through one nostril than through the other.
4. Feel how your lungs fill up as you inhale and how your chest relaxes when you exhale.
5. Now concentrate your attention on yourself as you observe your own breathing. Note that the observer, the Self, is different from the breathing that is being observed. You may explicitly tell yourself: 'I am not my breathing.'
6. Focus again on your breathing. Don't try to control it or deepen it, just become aware of it.
7. Become aware of the movements taking place in your body, your lungs, and your diaphragm. Become aware of your inhaling … and your exhaling. Say to yourself, 'I'm now drawing in the air … I'm now letting go of the air.' Without thinking. Just be aware.

FOCUS

• An excellent way to remedy distractions in prayer is to perceive images, memories, or thoughts when they arise, realising that the act of thinking is different from the Self that is thinking.

• Becoming aware of one's own breathing or bodily sensations leads to interior silence. God's revealed word is understood only in silence.

•This exercise quiets the mind and opens the way to wisdom and silence.

CONTEMPLATION

God Loves Us

1. God is father (2 Cor 6:18): 'I will be your father, and you shall be my sons and daughters, says the Lord Almighty.'

2. God tells of his love (Is 43-44):

'Do not fear, for I have redeemed you';

'I have called you by name, you are mine';

'you are precious in my sight';

'[you are] honoured and I love you';

'do not fear for I am with you';

'whom I created for my glory';

'Do not remember the former things, or consider the things of old; I have swept away your transgressions like a cloud, and your sins like a mist';

'return to me for I have redeemed you.'

3. The proof that God loves us is the sending of God's Son (1 Jn 4:9-10): 'God's love was revealed among us in this way: God sent his only Son into the world so that we might live through him. In this is love, not that we loved God but that he loved us and sent his Son to be the atoning sacrifice for our sins.'

4. The father also gives the Spirit to human beings (Lk 11:13): '… how much more will the Father give the Holy Spirit to those who ask him!'

5. We are called adopted children (1 Jn 3:1): 'See what love the Father has given us, that we should be called children of God; and that is what we are.'

6. The Father gives us life through Jesus Christ: The Father is the one who gives us life through Jesus. It was Jesus Christ himself who said: 'I came that they may have life and have it abundantly' (Jn 10:10). 'God gave us eternal life, and this life is in his Son' (1 Jn 5:11).

7. The Father is rich in mercy (Lk 15:11-32): Parable of the Prodigal Son.

3

Bodily Sensations: Serenity

1. Carry out and deepen exercise number 1, perceiving your bodily sensations from head to foot.
2. Try to become aware of the sensations in your head. If you feel some discomfort, become aware of it and relax until it goes away.
3. The five senses are in some fashion centred in the head. Gently close your eyes to heighten the sounds entering your ears, those far away and those close by.
4. Now move down to the sensations in your neck, the place where tensions usually accumulate. Try to relax your neck and your shoulders.
5. Feel your chest. Feel the clothes over it, over your stomach, over your abdomen. Feel the beating of your heart.
6. Become aware of the sensations in your right arm … in your left arm … in your right hand … in your left hand.
7. Now focus on your legs: your right leg … your left leg. Feel your legs, moving down, and then coming back up.
8. Finally feel your feet, loose or tight inside your shoes. Your right foot … your left foot.
9. Try to experience the serenity and the silence of your whole body. Rest in complete inner silence.

FOCUS

• Keep perfectly motionless: if you have bites, itching, and so forth, sense them only until they go away.

• The exercise above can be practised during the day, while walking, feeling the movement in the arms or in the legs … and so forth.

CONTEMPLATION

Being More

1. We are created in God's image (Gen 1:27): 'So God created humankind in his image.' Humans must freely complete the imperfect image of God that they are.

2. Jesus grew (Lk 2:52): 'Jesus grew in wisdom, and in years and in divine and human favour.'

3. Be perfect (Mt 5:48): 'Be perfect therefore as your heavenly Father is perfect.'

4. The visible image of the invisible God is Jesus Christ: Christ is 'the way, and the truth, and the life' (Jn 14:6). 'And this is eternal life, that they may know you, the only true God, and Jesus Christ whom you have sent' (Jn 17:3). 'I have come that they may have life, and have it abundantly' (Jn 10:10).

5. Paul's joy in having had a noble ideal (2 Tim 4:6-9): 'As for me, I am already being poured out as a libation, and the time of my departure has come. I have fought the good fight, I have finished the race, I have kept the faith. From now on there is reserved for me the crown of righteousness ...'

6. Jesus does the will of the Father (Heb 10:7): 'See, God, I have come to do your will'; 'Did you not know that I must be in my Father's house?' (Lk 2:49); 'My hour has not yet come' (Jn 2:5); 'The hour has come for the Son of Man to be glorified' (Jn 12:23); 'It is for this reason that I have come to this hour' (Jn 12:27); 'My food is to do the will of him who sent me and to complete his work' (Jn 4:34); 'My Father, if it is possible, let this cup pass from me; yet not what I want but what you want' (Mt 26:39).

7. Jesus has completely fulfilled the Father's plan (Lk 23:46): 'Father, into your hands I commend my spirit.' 'It is finished' (Jn 19:30).

Growth

The master used to assert the great idea
that in this matter of growth
all should go at their own pace.
He used to illustrate this theory
by telling his students this:
Someone saw a butterfly
struggling to get out of its cocoon …
The process of emergence was painful
and slow for someone watching.
So the man began
to blow his friendly warm breath
on the little bug
to help it emerge.
Indeed, he hastened things
and the butterfly was born,
but its tiny wings
ended up atrophied!
The master then finished by saying:
'In growth, my friends, things
cannot be hastened – to do so is disastrous.
Hastened growth will end up aborted!'

4

Breathing God

1. Return to exercise number 2. Concentrate again on your breathing. Become aware of the fact: the air entering, the air leaving. Warm air, cool air. The air filling your lungs, the air going out.
2. Reflect on deeper levels: the atmosphere is charged with God's presence. Inhale God as you inhale the air. As you inhale the air that supplies oxygen to your blood, feel how God also enters into you, how God purifies, renews, and fortifies.
3. The outgoing air is a polluted current, carrying off the impurities there. It carries away selfishness, cowardice. As it is replaced, you are filled with love, strength, and goodness.
4. Exhaling the air may be thought of as sending out acts of praise, thanksgiving, grace, energy, love, and forgiveness.

FOCUS

• In doing relaxation exercises, we avoid thoughts, but rather simply observe, as though we were beside a flowing river, or rolling ocean waves.

• These and other relaxation and silence exercises which lead us to feel God's presence within us may already be true prayer and may be extended at will.

CONTEMPLATION

Let Yourselves Be Reconciled

1. Sin in the bible: The biblical story is not always edifying: Adam's sin (Gen 3:1-24); Cain's sin (Gen 4:1-6); David's sin (2 Sam 11-12); Judas's sin (Jn 13:21-30).

2. Sin is against God's holiness (Bar 1:15-17): 'Justice is with the

Lord, our God: and we today are flushed with shame ... that we
... have sinned in the Lord's sight ...'

3. Sin is idolatry (Bar 1:22): '...but each one of us went off after the
devices of our own wicked hearts, served other gods, and did
evil in the sight of the Lord, our God.'

4. Sin is slavery (Bar 2:5): 'We are brought low, not raised up, because we sinned against the Lord, our God, not heeding his
voice.'

5. Sin is loneliness and exile (Bar 3:8): 'Behold us today in our cap-
tivity, where you scattered us, a reproach, a curse, and a requital
for all the misdeeds of our fathers, who withdrew from the Lord,
our God.'

6. We are all sinners (1 Jn 1:8-10): 'If we say that we have no sin,
we deceive ourselves, and the truth is not in us. If we confess our
sins, he who is faithful and just will forgive us our sins and
cleanse us from all unrighteousness. If we say that we have not
sinned, we make him a liar, and his word is not in us.'

7. But sin does not have the last word (Eph 2:4-5): 'But God, who is
rich in mercy, out of the great love with which he loved us even
when we were dead through our trespasses, made us alive together with Christ – by grace you have been saved.'

*One of the most disconcerting (and at the same time most delightful)
points of the master's teachings was this: God is closer to sinners than
to saints ... Here is how he explained that idea:*
God, up there, in heaven, is holding on to each person with a
string. Every time you sin, you cut the string; but God fixes the
string again, with a love knot. Since this knot makes the string
shorter, you are also a bit closer to God. Thus each sin cuts it,
and each cut means a knot, and each knot draws you closer to
God.

5

Breathing God: Wordless Communication

1. Repeat exercise number 2. Concentrate again on your breathing. Become aware of the air entering your lungs … and the air leaving.
2. Note your diaphragm filling and emptying.
3. Inhale and exhale several times gently. Feel the air going through your nose and being exhaled through your mouth. Warm air … cool air.
4. Focus your attention on yourself, on the Self that is breathing. Feel how the 'Self' is different from the breathing. You may say, 'I am not my breathing.'
5. The air is charged with God's presence. Inhale God as you inhale air. Express desire, hunger, and thirst for God.
6. Desire that he permeate and purify you, as the air that invades your lungs purifies your blood. As the air that gives your blood oxygen, God's presence is refreshing and energising.
7. Inhale deeply, desiring that God purify your life and fill it with goodness.
8. In exhaling the air, express repentance for your sins and omissions. Experience also the desire to surrender yourself. Put emphasis on this surrender as you exhale air from your lungs.
9. Consciously repeat inhalings and exhalings, giving them the meaning of surrender, love, familiarity, praise, thanksgiving, adoration, purification, and forgiveness. St Ignatius used to recommend this kind of rhythmic prayer combined with breathing.

- Our desires for God are acts of love.
- This and other exercises can purify us, as the act of contrition purifies, depending on our faith and God's grace.
- The experience of feeling that one is a sinner is true and salvific, if it is the experience of the love of God who frees humankind from sin. The experience of this prayer is that of seeing oneself purified, saved by the love of Jesus, who poured out his blood on the cross for all.
- Knowledge of sin, if true, is the work of the Holy Spirit, and never leads us to discouragement. It is a certainty of feeling that we are purified by God's love in Jesus Christ. 'The fact that I make known to you your sins is a clear sign that I want to heal you' (Pascal).

CONTEMPLATION

God Is Rich in Mercy

1. We have an advocate, Christ (1 Jn 2:1-2): 'My little children, I am writing these things to you so that you may not sin. But if anyone does sin, we have an advocate with the Father, Jesus Christ the righteous; and he is the atoning sacrifice for our sins, and not for ours only but also for the sins of the whole world.'

2. The lost sheep is found (Lk 15:3-7): 'So he told them this parable: "Which one of you, having a hundred sheep and losing one of them, does not leave the ninety-nine in the wilderness and go after the one that is lost until he finds it? When he has found it, he lays it on his shoulders and rejoices. And when he comes home, he calls together his friends and neighbours, saying to them, 'Rejoice with me, for I have found my sheep that was lost.'" Just so, I tell you, there will be more joy in heaven over one sinner who repents than over ninety-nine righteous persons who need no repentance.'

3. Jesus is the Good Shepherd (Jn 10:11, 14, 17): 'I am the good shepherd. The good shepherd lays down his life for the sheep. I am

the good shepherd. I know my own and my own know me ...
For this reason the Father loves me, because I lay down my life
in order to take it up again.'

4. *A new heart (Ez 36:25-26):* 'I will sprinkle clean water upon
you, and you shall be clean from all your uncleanness, and from
all your idols I will cleanse you. A new heart I will give you and
a new spirit I will put within you; and I will remove from your
body the heart of stone and give you a heart of flesh.'

5. *Put off the old man (Eph 4:22-24):* 'You were taught to put away
your former way of life, your old self, corrupt and deluded by its
lusts, and to be renewed in the spirit of your minds, and to
clothe yourself with the new self, created according to the likeness of God in true righteousness and holiness.'

Lost Sheep

A sheep found a hole in the fence and got out through it,
happy to find itself, at last, set free.
It walked for a long time and lost the way back home.
Only then did it see
that a hungry wolf was following it close behind.
The sheep ran and the wolf ran even more
until the shepherd arrived in time, and saved the animal,
and took it home very tenderly.
And against the advice of his friends
who saw what happened,
the shepherd refused to close up the hole
in the fence through which the sheep had fled, because, he said,
'It must be guaranteed its freedom!'

At Christ's Feet

At the feet of Christ crucified
let me ask, with Ignatius of Loyola:
What have I done for Christ?
What am I doing for Christ?
What must I do for Christ?

6

Bodily Sensations: In the Heart of Christ

1. Try the same bodily sensations exercise with something new.
2. Stop at each part of your body for a few seconds, trying to sense your scalp, forehead, eyelashes, nose, lips, cheeks, chin, neck, ears, shoulders, chest, torso, arms, hands, legs, feet … Look for more delicate and subtle sensations, for example, those in the area near your eyes.
3. Now reverse the process starting with your feet. Then settle your awareness on your body as a whole, without focusing on different parts, and feeling it alive with millions of sensations.
4. Now go beyond mere physical sensations. Think that each sensation is a biochemical reaction that needs the creative action of God almighty in order to exist.
5. Imagine this infinite power of God acting in you. Imagine what you feel each time you experience these sensations … Imagine that each of them is a loving touch from God, gentle, pleasant.
6. Imagine that this touch of God is luminous and health giving, that it soothes and heals everything.
7. You are now physically and psychologically ready to begin prayer on conversion. Listen to Jesus preaching in the public squares, the fields, the synagogues. He is beginning his apostolic preaching and his favourite topic is this: 'Repent and believe in the good news' (Mk 1:15).
8. Follow the preaching of this young prophet, full of new things, promises, and demands. 'He taught them as one having authority' (Mt 7:29). Hear the murmuring of the crowds who follow Jesus. Listen to Jesus speaking out loud.
9. Tell Jesus your past. Sit down with Jesus under a tree. Tell him about your whole past. It has been a little like that of the Prodigal Son, like the Lost Sheep. But Jesus does not really

care much about your past. He is at home with sinners; he sees hope in them, and they find fulfilment in his salvation.

10. Experience that the only thing remaining from the past, that which is most valid, is the experience of God's goodness and mercy: 'God has been good to me.' Now I know from experience that 'the Son of Man came to seek out and to save the lost' (Lk 19:10).

11. Enter into the heart of Christ. The present belongs to Christ. Ask for grace to enter into the heart of Christ and to feel how he loves us. We can say: 'I believe in his love, I am experiencing his love now, and I tell him, who is at my side: "I believe, Jesus, in your love".'

FOCUS

• As we practise these exercises, we naturally become better.

• Experience will gradually show that there is a great unity between the various exercises and that some of them suggest others.

• Be very free in your practice. Pursue those that are best adapted to you as an individual. Experience shows that normally five or ten minutes are sufficient for attaining the best results

CONTEMPLATION

New Life in Christ

1. New life in Christ (Eph 2:1-10): 'You were dead through the trespasses and sins in which you once lived, following the course of this world, following the ruler of the power of the air, the spirit that is now at work among those who are disobedient. All of us once lived among them in the passions of our flesh and senses, and we were by nature children of wrath, like everyone else. But God, who is rich in mercy, out of the great love with which he loved us even when we were dead through our trespasses, made us alive together with Christ – by grace you have been saved – and raised us up with him and seated us with him in the heavenly places in Christ Jesus, so that in the ages to come he might show the immeasurable riches of his grace in kindness towards us in Christ Jesus. For by grace you have been saved through faith, and this is not your own doing; it is the gift of God – not the result of works so that no one may boast. For we are what he has made us, created in Christ Jesus for good works, which God prepared beforehand to be our way of life.'

2. *Behold I make all new (Is 43:18-19):* 'Do not remember the former things, or consider the things of old. I am now about to do a new thing; now it springs forth, do you not perceive it? I will make a way in the wilderness and rivers in the desert.'

'I, I am he who blots out your transgressions for my own sake, and I will not remember your sins' (Is 43:25).

'I have swept away your transgressions like a cloud, and your sins like mist; return to me, for I have redeemed you' (Is 44:22).

3. *A new heart (Ez 36:26):* 'A new heart I will give you, and a new spirit I will put within you; and I will remove from your body the heart of stone and give you a heart of flesh.'

Oh Happy Fault!

The Jewish mystic Baal Shem used to pray to God
in a very curious way. He spoke like this:
'Remember, Lord, that you need
me as much as I need you.
If you didn't exist
to whom would I pray?
And if I didn't exist
who would pray to you?'
It has brought me great joy to think that had I not sinned,
God would have no reason to show his mercy.
He needs my sin.
There really is more joy in heaven
over a sinner who repents
than over ninety-nine who have need of repentance.

7

A Place to Pray: Vision of God in Nature

1. The vision. Withdraw in your imagination to some site propitious for creating a climate of silence and praise: the beach, a mountaintop, a riverbank, a church in silence, a flat rooftop under a starry sky.

2. Open your eyes to contemplate nature around you: trees, birds, animals, the sky, the mountains, the city, people. Contemplate still nature and draw in the silence that it transmits.

3. Look also at nature in movement: early morning cool, mid-day heat, colours of sunset, darkness of the night, the stars, the moon.

4. Ask nature, the trees, birds, rivers, mountains, stars if they have some message to offer. Especially ask the people what they have to say.

   > Oh, valleys and woods,
   > planted by the hand of the beloved,
   > tell if he has passed by you!
   > – *St John of the Cross*

5. Also ask the Lord what he has to say through nature. Wait for God's response. It may be a word, a phrase, or silence.

6. Ponder the fact that through your eyes God contemplates the beauty of creation. Invite God to see through your eyes the most beautiful things that God has created. Should you feel inspired, with the bible, invite creation to glorify the Lord with the song of Dan 3:52-90.

• This exercise may have new and rich connotations if done in special circumstances, for example, at sunrise, facing the sea, on a mountain top, in a beautiful park full of birds singing, feeling the rain come down.

• It is a wonderful way for creatures to be elevated to the creator.

CONTEMPLATION
Conversion of Zacchaeus

1. Zacchaeus was not satisfied (Lk 19:1- 4): Jesus 'entered Jericho and was passing through it. A man was there named Zacchaeus; he was a chief tax collector and he was rich. He was trying to see who Jesus was, but on account of the crowd he could not, because he was short of stature. So he ran ahead and climbed a sycamore tree to see him, because he was going to pass that way.'

2. Jesus takes the initiative of going to his house (Lk 19:5): 'When Jesus came to the place, he looked up and said to him, "Zacchaeus, hurry and come down; for I must stay at your house today."'

3. Zacchaeus receives Jesus in his home (Lk 19:6): 'So he hurried down and was happy to welcome him.'

4. The Pharisees understand nothing of the mystery of grace (Lk 19:7): 'All who saw it began to grumble and said, "He has gone to be the guest of one who is a sinner."'

5. Radical conversion of Zacchaeus (Lk 19:8): 'Zacchaeus stood there and said to the Lord, "Look, half of my possessions, Lord, I will give to the poor; and if I have defrauded anyone of anything, I will pay back four times as much."'

6. Joy of Jesus over the spiritual healing of Zacchaeus (Lk 19:9-10): 'Then Jesus said to him, "Today salvation has come to this house, because he too is a son of Abraham. For the Son of Man came to seek out and to save the lost."'

7. New life in Christ (Rom 12:2): 'Do not be conformed to this world, but be transformed by the renewing of your minds, so that you may discern what is the will of God – what is good and acceptable and perfect.'

God has forgotten

Once a woman who thought she was having visions of God
 went to the bishop for advice.
He suggested, 'You may be believing in illusions.
You must realise that as bishop of the diocese,
I am the one to decide whether your visions are true or false.'
'Yes, your excellency.'
'That's my responsibility, my duty.'
'Of course, your excellency.'
'So you must do what I say.'
'I will, your excellency.'
'Then listen: the next time God appears to you
as you say he does, you are to perform a test
by which to know that it is really God.'
'Agreed, your excellency. But what is the test?'
'Say to God, "Please, tell me the personal
and private sins of the bishop."
If it is God who is appearing to you,
he will reveal my sins. Then come back here and tell me,
and no one else. Agreed?'
'I'll do it, your excellency.'
After a month she requested to see the bishop,
who asked her: 'Did God appear to you again?'
'I think so, your excellency.'
'What did God say?'
'God said to me, "Go tell the bishop that
I've forgotten all his sins."'
What's this? No book for recording sins.
Want to know something?
God does not keep any registry, any log.
He sees us in the present movement,
and enfolds us in an unsurpassable love.

8

EXERCISE

Hearing Sounds – And God's Voice in Them

1. Listen to the sounds around you. All of them: those closet ... those furthest away ... the softest ... the loudest. First try to identify each sound. Don't think about them, just feel them.
2. Now listen to these sounds not separately, but as a totality as though they made up a symphony filling the universe. They are signs of the life existing around you. Feel yourself in communion with all these sounds. Invite them to glorify the Lord.
3. Imagine that you are lending God your ears so that God may also hear this symphony arising out of creation itself.
4. Invite God to pay attention to the most pleasant sounds of the nature that God has created. Rest in the thought that God is listening through your ears.
5. Listen to what God tells you in the sounds of nature.

FOCUS

• There is a silence at the centre of each sound. Sounds are distracting when we want to repeat them or flee from them.

• We can transform sounds, for everything depends on how we receive them. Complete harmony is possible, depending on each one of us.

• Each sound has dozens of sounds within it: try to recognise them all.

CONTEMPLATION

On the Mountain with Jesus

1. *Our will:* Arrange to meet with Jesus on the mountain top. In his presence and with his grace, write a kind of will. Fill it out point by point, striving to be completely open with Jesus:

- These persons have been dear to me in life ...
- These ideas and experiences have brought me liberation ...
- I have lived for these things ...
- This has been my vision:

  Of the Father ...

  Of Jesus Christ: 'Who do you say that I am?' ...

  Of Mary ...

  Of the church ...

- These are the dangers with which I have flirted in my life ...
- These are the sufferings that have matured me ...
- These are the influences that have shaped my life (persons, occupations, books, events) ...
- These are the biblical texts that have shed light on my path ...
- These are the events of my life for which I repent ...
- These are the things for which I must continually be thankful to God ...
- These are the graces that I want to attain in this prayer ...
- I want to liberate myself from these things ...

2. *Clothed in the New Self (Eph 4:22-24):* 'You were taught to put away your former way of life, your old self, corrupt and deluded by its lusts, and to be renewed in the spirit of your minds, and to clothe yourselves with the new self, created according to the likeness of God in true righteousness and holiness.'

3. *And you shall be clean (Ez 36:25):* 'I will sprinkle clean water upon you, and you shall be clean from all your uncleanness, and from all your idols I will cleanse you.'

9

Listening to God, Hearing the Word

1. Repeat exercise 8. Become aware of the sounds around you, becoming aware that hearing is an activity in itself, that the 'listening' is one thing and that the 'Self' listening is another.

2. Consider: each sound is produced and sustained by God Almighty. God is 'sound'. Repose in the world of sounds. Repose in God.

3. There is no need for special thoughts, or intuitions: simply with full clarity become aware of the hearing, of the 'Self,' and you will be on your way back home, returning to yourself.

4. Your 'Self' will remain in silence and God will not be far off. Saint Augustine says that human beings must turn upon themselves in order to make themselves a stepping stone for turning to God.

5. Feel the message that God offers in each sound. Each sound is a touch of God, gentle, pleasant, soothing, harmonious .

6. Finally, go down into the depths of the heart to find there 'that special Word' that God wants to say, here and now. Listen to 'that Word': Jesus. He is the Word. Soft in the beginning, but gradually building up volume. Feel how it impacts on your whole being, head, heart, members.

7. Do not pronounce this Word, but just listen to it, rejoicing to note that it makes you happy. That it brings you peace and harmonises your being.

8. Now look at how 'the Word' breaks the barriers of your being and spreads into the world around you. Starting with you, it spreads into the whole world like a sound wave.

9. See how each creature vibrates in tune with this Word: plants, birds, sea, stars, sun, mountains and valleys, human beings, angels vibrate in tune with this Word. In it everything is unified and harmonised, everything becomes pure and beautiful. Everything takes on its meaning.

10. Shout that Word within yourself with all your strength and whenever the Spirit inspires you.

• Practising these exercises over time produces surprising effects: the fruit of the silence we are learning to find.

• This silence opens space for the action of the Spirit who acts and shouts in our hearts. This silence is the place where the Spirit is found within us. It has much to tell us about the one whom the Father has sent us.

CONTEMPLATION

The Reign of God

1. Peter's journey – first encounter with Jesus: Before Peter came to be able to profess his love for Jesus on the lakeside with humility and truth, he had to pass through a long preparatory journey which can be a model for our surrender to Jesus Christ. 'As he walked by the Sea of Galilee, he saw two brothers, casting a net into the sea – for they were fishermen. And he said to them, "Follow me, and I will make you fish for people." Immediately they left their nets and followed him.'

2. Peter's first dialogue with Jesus (Lk 5:8, 10-11): When Peter saw the miraculous catch of fish, 'he fell down at Jesus' knees, saying, "Go away from me, Lord, for I am a sinful man!" Then Jesus said to Simon, "Do not be afraid; from now on you will be catching people." When they had brought their boats to shore, they left everything and followed him.'

3. Peter's second dialogue with Jesus (Mt 14:26-31): 'When the disciples saw him walking on the sea, they were terrified, saying "It is a ghost!" and they cried out in fear. But immediately Jesus spoke to them and said, "Take heart, it is I; do not be afraid." Peter answered him, "Lord, if it is you, command me to come to you on the water." He said "Come." So Peter got out of the boat, started walking on the water, and came toward Jesus. But when he noticed the strong wind, he became frightened, and beginning to sink, he cried out, "Lord save me!" Jesus immediately reached out his hand and caught him, saying to him, "You of little faith, why did you doubt?"'

4. *Peter's confession, which earns him first place (Mt 16:13-18):* Jesus 'asked his disciples, "Who do people say that the Son of Man is?" And they said, "Some say John the Baptist, but others Elijah, and still others Jeremiah or one of the prophets." He said to them, "But who do you say that I am?" Simon Peter answered, "You are the Messiah, the Son of the living God." And Jesus answered him, "Blessed are you, Simon son of Jonah! For flesh and blood has not revealed this to you, but my Father in heaven. And I tell you, you are Peter, and on this rock I will build my church."'

5. *Jesus' exchange with Peter at the washing of the feet (Jn 13:6-9):* 'He came to Simon Peter, who said to him, "Lord are you going to wash my feet?" Jesus answered, "You do not know now what I am doing, but later you will understand." Peter said to him, "You will never wash my feet." Jesus answered, "Unless I wash you, you have no share with me." Simon Peter said to him, "Lord, not my feet only but also my hands and my head."'

6. *Prediction of Peter's denial (Jn 13:36-38):* 'Simon Peter said to him, "Lord, where are you going?" Jesus answered, "Where I am going, you cannot follow me now; but you will follow afterward." Peter said to him. "Lord why can I not follow you now? I will lay down my life for you." Jesus answered, "Will you lay down your life for me? Very truly, I tell you, before the clock crows, you will have denied me three times."'

7. *What seemed impossible has happened with Peter (Mt 26:73-75):* 'After a little while the bystanders came up and said to Peter, "Certainly you are also one of them, for your accent betrays you." Then he began to curse, and he swore an oath, "I do not know the man!" Then Peter remembered what Jesus had said: "Before the cock crows, you will deny me three times." And he went out and wept bitterly.' Luke adds an extremely important detail after the third denial: 'At the moment, while he was still speaking, the cock crowed. The Lord turned and looked at Peter. Then

Peter remembered the word of the Lord, how he had said to him, "Before the cock crows today, you will deny me three times." And he went out and wept bitterly.'

8. *From love for Christ to the primacy of Peter (Jn 21:15-17):* 'When they had finished breakfast, Jesus said to Simon Peter, "Simon son of John, do you love me more than these?" He said to him, "Yes, Lord; you know that I love you." Jesus said to him, "Feed my lambs." A second time he said to him, "Simon son of John, do you love me?" "Yes, Lord; you know that I love you." Jesus said to him, "Tend my sheep." He said to him the third time, "Simon son of John, do you love me?" Peter felt hurt because he said to him the third time, "Do you love me?" And he said to him, "Lord, you know everything; you know that I love you." Jesus said to him, "Feed my sheep."'

Salt Figurine

The salt figurine wandered over the earth
until it came to the sea, where it remained lost
in contemplation of that huge mass
of swirling water that it had never seen.
'Who are you?' it finally asked the sea.
'Come on in and see,' said the sea with a smile.
Without further ado, it entered the sea,
and the deeper it went, the more it dissolved
until only a tiny amount of its body was left.
Just before being completely dissolved,
the figurine exclaimed,
'Now I know who you are!'

10

Returning to the World of the Senses

1. Return now to the world of the senses. Hush any words and thoughts. Become aware of the sounds around you ... those closet, those furthest away. The most pleasant, the least pleasant.
2. Feel the sensations in your body ... weary ... aching ... relaxed ...
3. Become aware of your breathing ... calm ... nervous ...
4. Now detect God: in the sounds heard ... in sensations present.
5. Surrender to God in your exhalation. Receive God in your inhaling.
6. Feel at peace, at ease with God's presence flooding your whole being.
7. Repeat exercise 9, points 6 to 10.

FOCUS

• By now we know from experience the kind of climate that we must create for prayer, properly speaking, by means of the various 'exercises'.

• If, in order to create this climate, we still feel the need, we may repeat any of the previous exercises whose effect we have already experienced.

CONTEMPLATION

Who Do You Say That I Am?

1. *Jesus is simple:* He is born poor: 'She gave birth to her firstborn son and wrapped him in bands of cloth, and laid him in a manger, because there was no place for them in the inn' (Lk 2:&); he is first visited by the poor: 'When the angels had left them and gone into heaven, the shepherds said to one another, "Let us go to Bethlehem and see this thing that has taken place"' (Lk 2:15); his family was from among the poor: 'Is not this the carpenter's son?' (Mt 13:55); like the head of a household issuing an invitation, he surrounds himself with poor people: 'Go out at once onto the streets and lanes of the town and bring in the poor, the crippled, the blind, and the lame' (Lk 14:21); he calls them blessed: 'Blessed are you who are poor, for yours is the kingdom of God' (Lk 6:20); most of the apostles are fishermen: Jesus 'saw Simon and his brother Andrew casting a net into the sea – for they were fishermen. And Jesus said to them, "Follow me and I will make you fish for people"' (Mk 1:16-17), and 'As he went a little farther, he saw James son of Zebedee and his brother John, who were in their boat mending the nets. Immediately he called them ...' (Mk1: 19-20); he comes to bring good news to the poor: 'The Spirit of the Lord is upon me, because he has anointed me to bring good news to the poor.' (Lk 4:18); he does not have any place to lay his head: 'Foxes have holes, and birds of the air have nests; but the Son of Man has nowhere to lay his head' (Mt 8:20); he wastes time with children, 'People were bringing little children to him in order that he might touch them; and the disciples spoke sternly to them. But when Jesus saw this, he was indignant and said to them, "Let the little children come to me; do not stop them: for it is to such as these that the kingdom of God belongs. Truly I tell you, whoever does not receive the kingdom of God as a little child will never enter it." And he took them up in his arms, laid his hands on them, and blessed them' (Mk 10:13-16); he praises the Father because he has revealed the mysteries of the kingdom to the simple: 'I thank you, Father, Lord of heaven

and earth, because you have hidden these things from the wise and the intelligent and have revealed them to infants' (Lk 10:21).

2. Jesus devotes special attention to the poor and the sick: He moves to heal the crippled woman (Lk 13:12); he has mercy on the leper (Lk 5:12-16); he heals a paralytic (Lk 5:17-26); he heals the centurion's servant (Lk 7:1-10); he heals the woman who has touched the fringe of his clothes (Lk 8:43-48); he heals ten lepers (Lk 17:11-19); he heals the blind man of Jericho (Lk 18:35-43); he raises the only son of the widow of Nain (Lk 7:11-17); he raises the daughter of Jairus (Lk 8:40-56); he raises Lazarus (Jn 11:1-44).

3. Jesus knows how to be a friend: 'As the Father has loved me, so I have loved you; abide in my love' (Jn 15:9); 'One of his disciples – the one whom Jesus loved – was reclining next to him' (Jn 13:23); 'I do not call you servants ... but I have called you friends because I have made known to you everything that I have heard from my Father' (Jn 15:15); 'Jesus loved Martha and her sister and Lazarus' (Jn 11:5).

4. Jesus is kind and sensitive: He orders that the girl whom he has restored to life be given something to eat (Lk 8:55); he admires the noble act of the poor widow (Lk 21:4); he is sensitive to the beauty of the lilies (Lk 12:27); after days of wearying apostolate he asks the apostles to rest: 'Come away to a deserted place all by yourselves and rest a while' (Mk 6:31).

5. He reveals his kind heart toward sinners with words and deeds:

• Words: parable of the Prodigal Son (Lk 15;11-32); parable of the lost sheep (Lk 15:1-7); parable of the lost coin (Lk 15:8-10); parable of the Good Samaritan (Lk 10:29-37).

• Deeds: he forgives the sinful woman because of her great love (Lk 7:36-50); he visits the house of Zacchaeus, who is converted (Lk 19:1-10); the conversation at Jacob's well converts the Samaritan woman (Lk 4:1-42); he forgives the adulterous woman (Lk 8:1-11). 'Now all the tax collectors and sinners were coming near to listen to him. And the Pharisees and the scribes were grumbling and saying, "This fellow welcomes sinners and eats with them."' (Lk 15:1-2).

6. Jesus is he who values and inspires others: Speaking of John the

Baptist he said: 'I tell you among those born of women no one is greater than John' (Lk 7:28); speaking of the disciples he says, 'You are the salt of the earth ... You are the light of the world' (Mt 5:13-14); Jesus rejoices over the apostolic success of the seventy-two disciples (Lk 10:17-20).

7. *Jesus is Son of God:* greater than Abraham (Jn 8:58) and Moses (Mt 19:8-9); more than David (Mt 12:23); more than Solomon (Mt 12:42): more than Jonah (Mt 12:41); more than John the Baptist (Jn 1:27) and than any other prophet; he has authority over the law (Mt 5:27-33) and acts on the Sabbath (Mk 2:28); he says he is able to raise and grant immortality to the human being (Jn 5:21 and 6:44); he does the works of the Father (Jn 10:36-37); he is one with the Father (Jn 10:30, 38).

Christ at the centre of all

All things were formed in him, through him and for him:
He is the image of God invisible,
Firstborn of the entire creation
because all things were created in him,
in heaven and on earth, the visible and the invisible,
thrones, dominions, authorities, powers,
all was created through him and for him.
He existed before all and all things hold together in him.
And he is also Head of the Body, that is, of the church.
He is the beginning,
the Firstborn among the dead,
so that he may have the first place among all things.
For it has pleased God that all fullness should dwell in him,
and also, through Christ,
to reconcile to himself everything there is,
both in the heavens, and on earth,
making peace through the blood of his cross.

– Col 1:15-20

11

EXERCISE

Praying with the Body

1. St Paul asks, 'Do you not know that you are God's temple and that God's spirit dwells in you?' (1 Cor 3:16). And the psalmist presents the body as 'the faithful collaborator and expression of our feelings' (See Ps 69:3).
2. Become aware that body and spirit make up a praying unit that can say with St Augustine, 'You have created me, Lord, for yourself, and my heart is restless until rests in you.'
3. Rejoice in this reality, and while standing, lift up your hands, expressing with your entire 'Self' body-spirit, your thirst for the living God.
4. Express spontaneously, through bodily gestures your deepest feelings: wonder, satisfaction, joy, reverence, praise, adoration, thanksgiving.
5. Find the way to express in gestures, with your hands, with looking, all these and other feelings that are welling up at this moment: sorrow, trust in God, surrender.

FOCUS

• Prayer techniques are a means, not an end. If we attribute too much importance to the techniques, prayer becomes a sheer exercise for becoming physically or psychologically relaxed and nothing more.

• The body is part of our being and we must use it to become interiorly recollected. It is we who are praying, 'soul and body' like Jesus, who while praying in the garden face down (Luke says: he 'knelt down'), offers this prayer: 'My Father, if it is possible, let this cup pass from me' (Mt 26:39).

• The bible and the liturgy situate the body at prayer. The masters of prayer say that 'prayer methods' are like a drawbridge for entering a castle. It is true that no human technique, Zen, or

yoga by itself attains the experience of God, union with God, contemplation. This goal of Christian prayer is sheer gift of God. It is as means that bodily and ascetical techniques acquire meaning. St Teresa used to say, 'We aren't angels, for we have a body.'
• Another great master of prayer, St Ignatius Loyola, recommends various body postures in the *Spiritual Exercises*: standing up, prostrate, kneeling, seated, lying down, and so forth, and one of his prayer methods is called 'application of the senses': sight, hearing, taste, smell, touch.

CONTEMPLATION
The Incarnation

1. The mystery of the Incarnation (Lk 1:26-38): We are now going to reflect with Mary who 'treasured all these things in her heart' (Lk 2:51).

2. See how the Blessed Trinity is involved in the mystery of the Incarnation (Gal 4:4-6): 'But when the fullness of time had come, God sent his Son, born of a woman ... so that we might receive adoption as children. And because you are children, God has sent the Spirit of his Son into our hearts, crying "Abba! Father!"'
'These are words celebrating together the love of the Father, the mission of the Son, the gift of the Holy Spirit, the woman of whom the Redeemer was born, and our divine filiation.' (RM).

3. See how the Father is involved in the mystery of the Incarnation (1 Jn 4:9-10): 'God's love was revealed among us in this way: God sent his only Son into the world so that we might live through him. In this is love, not that we loved God but that he loved us and sent his Son to be the atoning sacrifice for our sins.'
'He will be great and will be called the Son of the Most High ... therefore the child to be born will be holy; he will be called Son of God' (Lk 1:32, 35).

4. See how the Son is involved in the mystery of the Incarnation (Heb 10:5-7) 'Consequently when Christ came into the world, he said: "Sacrifices and offerings you have not desired, but a body you have prepared for me; in burnt offerings and sin offerings you have taken no pleasure." Then I said, "See, God, I have come to do your will, O God".'

'You will conceive in your womb and bear a son, and you will name him Jesus' (Lk 1:31).

'And the Word became flesh and lived among us' (Jn 1:14).

5. See how the Holy Spirit is involved in the mystery of the Incarnation (Lk 1:35): 'The Holy Spirit will come upon you, and the power of the Most High will overshadow you.'

'The Incarnation marks the moment when the Holy Spirit shaped the human nature of Christ in the virginal womb' (RM).

6. See how Mary takes part in the mystery of the Incarnation (Lk 1:30-31, 38): 'Do not be afraid, Mary, for you have found favour with God. And now you will conceive in your womb and bear a son, and you will name him Jesus' … Then Mary said, 'Here am I, the servant of the Lord; let it be with me according to your word.'

'But when the fullness of time had come, God sent his son, born of a woman.'

'The Incarnation of the Word, the hypostatic union of the Son of God with human nature, is achieved and consummated specifically in Mary' (RM).

7. See how human beings are involved in the mystery of the Incarnation (Gal 4:4-7): 'God sent his Son born of a woman, so that we might receive adoption as children.'

In the fullness of time

When the fullness of time had come,
God sent his Son,
born of a woman, born under the law,
in order to redeem those who were under the law,
and make us adoptive children.
And the proof that you are children
is that God has sent into our hearts
the spirit of his Son, crying, 'Abba! Father!'

— *Gal 4:4-6*

12

Subtler Sensations

1. Choose subtler bodily sensations, breathings, or sounds for the basic purpose of settling your attention. If your attention wanders from the central point, acknowledge that wandering: 'I am now thinking,' 'I am now bothered,' 'I am now listening.' Then gently shift to the basic object of attention. This can be repeated at any moment when you recognise distraction.

2. Sharpening your perception also helps. Choose subtler sensations, softer sounds, contact of the air passing through your nose.

3. You may also take a small part of your body, your fingers or toes, for example, and feel the sensations in them; or breathe, concentrating just on inhaling or on exhaling, if there are many bothersome distractions.

4. It doesn't matter if you don't feel anything in these parts of your body. The mere effort to experience sensations there will give you the benefit of this exercise. Silence cannot be induced or sought directly – what must be sought in itself is simply a state of attention to something concrete and silence will arise.

5. In order to communicate with God within this silence, imagine that you receive it each time you inhale, and that you surrender to it each time you exhale. Imagine that each inhalation of air corresponds to God's desire to give himself to you and that each exhalation is an expression of your desire to surrender to God. When you inhale, God says 'yes' to you, accepting yourself as you are now, with your past and your future. As you exhale, you surrender to God, you place yourself in God's hands and will, and everything will accordingly be in harmony and peace.

• These 'ways of praying' are quite packed and may take up days and days. We can be very free in sticking with them for a number of days.

• An important piece of advice from the author of the *Exercises*, Saint Ignatius: 'For it is not knowing a great deal that satiates and satisfies the soul, but feeling and savouring things intimately.'

CONTEMPLATION

The Visitation

1. Be present at Mary's journey to Ain-Karin (Lk 1:39-40): 'In those days, Mary set out and went with haste to a Judean town in the hill country, where she entered the house of Zechariah and greeted Elizabeth.'

'Prompted by charity, Mary goes to her relative's house' (RM).

2. Elizabeth's greeting (Lk 1:41-42): 'When Elizabeth heard Mary's greeting, the child leaped in her womb. And Elizabeth was filled with the Holy Spirit and exclaimed with a loud cry, "Blessed are you among women, and blessed is the fruit of your womb."'

'Elizabeth, in response to Mary's greeting, having felt the child in her own womb leap for joy, full of the Holy Spirit, exclaims with a loud cry, "Blessed are you among women, and blessed is the fruit of your womb." This proclamation and exclamation of Elizabeth has entered into the Hail Mary, continuing the angel's greeting' (RM).

3. Elizabeth witnesses to Mary (Lk 1:43): 'And why has this happened to me, that the mother of my Lord comes to me?'

'Elizabeth gives witness to Mary: she recognises and proclaims that before her stands the mother of the Lord, the Mother of the Messiah. The infant that Elizabeth bears in her womb also shares in this witness: "The child in my womb leaped for joy" (Lk 1:44)' (RM).

4. Happy she who has believed (Lk 1:45): 'And blessed is she who believed that there would be a fulfilment of what was spoken to her by the Lord.'

'This response of faith contains a perfect co-operation with divine grace and an openness to the action of the Holy Spirit. Mary pronounced her *fiat* through faith. It was through faith that she surrendered to God without reservation and dedicated herself wholeheartedly as a servant, to the person and work of her Son' (RM).

5. *Mary's song of praise (Lk 1:46-49):* 'My soul magnifies the Lord, and my spirit rejoices in God my Saviour, for he has looked with favour on the lowliness of his servant. Surely, from now on all generations will call me blessed; for the Mighty One has done great things for me, and holy is his name.'

'These sublime words, which are at the same time very simple and wholly inspired by sacred scripture, reveal Mary's personal experience, the ecstasy of her heart. She glorifies God, holy and almighty, source of all gifts, because in her he has done great things: through Mary God has given his Son to the world: God "so loved the world that he gave his only Son" (Jn 3:16), and hence "My spirit rejoices in God my Saviour"' (RM).

6. *Mary's preferential love for the poor (Lk 1:50-55):* 'His mercy is for those who fear him from generation to generation. He has shown strength with his arm; he has scattered the proud in the thoughts of their hearts. He has brought down the powerful from their thrones, and has lifted up the lowly; he has filled the hungry with good things, and sent the rich away empty. He has helped his servant Israel, in remembrance of his mercy, according to the promise he made to our ancestors, to Abraham and to his descendants forever.'

'The church is very much aware that the importance of the "poor" and the "option for the poor" in the word of the living God must be safeguarded. This is a theme connected to the "Christian meaning of freedom and of liberation." Mary, utterly dependent on God and entirely oriented to God, alongside her Son, is the "most perfect icon of the freedom and liberation" of humankind and of the cosmos. It is toward Mary that the church, for which she is Mother and model, must look in order to understand the meaning of its own mission in its entirety' (RM).

13

Praying Seated in Silence

1. Feel that you are seated at Jesus' feet like Mary, the sister of Martha and Lazarus. This is the position of one who wishes to listen and converse calmly, without haste. Mary 'sat at the Lord's feet and listened to what he was saying' (Lk 10:39). There are two preferred ways to be seated for prayer:

2. Seated Carmelite fashion: seated on your heels. The tips of your feet should be joined and your heels a little apart to get better support. Your arms should be extended and your hands supported on your thighs with your palms turned up. You may use a small platform or pillow. This position expresses acceptance, listening, attention.

3. Seated in a chair: sit up with your back straight. Keep your legs perpendicular to the floor. Have your feet a few centimetres apart in a stable position. Your arms may fall alongside your body, leaving your hands on your thighs with the palms upwards or down, or crossed in front of your body, or in some expressive position, as long as it isn't forced. This assures tranquility and peace and is the most common way to pray.

4. Withdraw in your imagination to any place where you have felt happy. Recall all the details: sight, sound, smell, taste, touch. Observe what you feel. Return to the present situation. What do you feel? Observe the contrast.

FOCUS

• We can check in the text of St Ignatius the important role of the senses (imagination) in this contemplation: seeing, hearing, and so forth.

• 'Withdrawing' provides strength for facing the current situation and heightens our perception of the present situation.

CONTEMPLATION
Birth of Jesus

1. The birth of Jesus (Lk 2:1-20): Without haste, calmly enter into contemplation of the birth of Jesus in Bethlehem.

'The time came for her to deliver her child. And she gave birth to her firstborn son and wrapped him in bands of cloth, and laid him in a manger, because there was no place for them in the inn.'

'I will see the persons: our Lady, and St Joseph, and the Child Jesus … I will look upon them, contemplating them, and ministering to their needs' *(Spiritual Exercises).*

2. I will listen to what the angel says: 'But the angel said to them, "Do not be afraid; for see – I am bringing you good news of great joy for all the people: to you is born this day in the city of David a Saviour, who is the Messiah, the Lord. This will be a sign for you: you will find a child wrapped in bands of cloth and lying in a manger." And suddenly there was with the angel a multitude of the heavenly host, praising God and saying, "Glory to God in the highest heaven, and on earth peace among those whom he favours!"' (Lk 2:10-14).

3. I will listen to what the shepherds say: 'Let us go now to Bethlehem and see this thing that has taken place, which the Lord has made known to us.'

4. I will listen and consider what they do: Mary takes care of the child, dresses him, nurses him. Joseph obtains shelter for the Mother and Child. There is a great deal of poverty, but a great deal of love, and happiness. Mary is trying to understand: 'Mary treasured all these words and pondered them in her heart' (Lk 2:19).

5. 'We declare to you what we have seen and heard so that you also may have fellowship with us; and truly our fellowship is with the Father and Son Jesus Christ. We are writing these things so that our joy may be complete' (1 Jn 1:3-4).

6. See how Jesus chooses the life of a poor person: 'For you know the generous act of our Lord Jesus Christ, that though he was rich, yet for your sakes he became poor, so that by his poverty you might become rich' (2 Cor 8:9).

14

Praying Standing Up

1. Praying standing up: it is a good idea to be standing for some contemplation. You may attempt that now. It is a common way of praying in the liturgy.

2. These are some of the meanings that the standing position may have:

    • Being alert, available, and ready to depart. It is a dynamic stance, the prelude to another. It is the situation of a solider hearing an order or an athlete ready to start a competition. Create that kind of availability toward God within you now.

    • Standing also indicates respect. That is why you maintain such a posture before someone representing authority. Create in yourself this feeling of respect for the presence of God.

    • Standing may also denote welcome: the same welcome that you show when you get up to embrace a friend who arrives. Welcome in your heart those persons you are going to be with today.

    • It may indicate joy. Fans in a stadium stand up every time the ball hits the opponent's goal. Strive now to grasp the reasons you have to be happy.

    • The bible often speaks about 'standing up': 'He said to me: O mortal, stand up on your feet, and I will speak with you. And when he spoke to me, a spirit entered into me and set me on my feet; and I heard him speaking to me!' (Ez 2:1-2).

FOCUS

• Some people prefer to go walking slowly, in a quiet place. This is another of the 'ways of praying.'

• This kind of prayer is always contemplation, born of a desire to know the Lord intimately. Contemplation leads us to take on deep thoughts and love for Christ.

CONTEMPLATION

Presentation of Jesus

1. Presentation of Jesus: Lk 2:23-24: See Mary and Joseph in the temple, among so many worshippers, dedicating their son. 'Every firstborn male shall be designated as holy to the Lord' (Lk 2:23).

• See that the sacrifice offering of the mother is that of a poor family. 'They offered ... a pair of turtledoves or two young pigeons' (Lk 2:24).

• Reflect on how Jesus incarnates himself in human life without accepting privileges: 'Is not this the carpenter's son?' (Mt 13:55).

2. The old man, Simeon (Lk 2:22-35): Refer to how the evangelist presents him: he 'was righteous and devout,'

• 'looking forward to the consolation of Israel,'

• 'the Holy Spirit rested on him.'

• 'It had been revealed to him by the Holy Spirit that he would not see death before he had seen the Lord's Messiah.'

• 'Guided by the Holy Spirit, Simeon came into the temple;'

• 'Simeon took him in his arms and praised God, saying, "Master, now you are dismissing your servant in peace, according to your word; for my eyes have seen your salvation, which you have prepared in the presence of all peoples, a light for revelation to the Gentiles and for glory to your people Israel".'

• Simeon foresees that Mary will undergo a long and painful separation from her child. 'This child is destined for the falling and the rising of many in Israel, and to be a sign that will be opposed so that the inner thoughts of many will be revealed – and a sword will pierce your own soul too.'

3. Part three: Anna's prophecy (Lk 2:36-38): Note how the evangelist presents Anna.

• 'She never left the temple,'

• she 'worshiped there day and night'

• 'with fasting and prayer;'

• 'she came and began to praise God'

• 'and to speak about the child to whom all who were looking for the redemption of Jerusalem.'

15

Peak Experience

1. Do a relaxation and silence exercise, possibly number 7.
2. Withdraw in your imagination to a place where you have had intense experience of God's presence. Recall this place as vividly as possible.
3. Try to relive that same experience in that very same environment. For some people it may have been an experience of contemplating nature, on a mountain top, while contemplating the sea, a dawn, or a sunset that has left its mark. Others have encountered God while on retreat or in a community action. Others have met God in a moment of joy, such as the birth of a child, or of sadness, such as the death of a family member. Relive if possible some of these moments of grace.
4. Return to the place and situation of this experience that has left its mark: what are your feelings? gratitude? praise?
5. Return to the present moment. Compare that experience of the past with the current moment.

FOCUS

• Many profound life experiences will be useful for preparing and nourishing prayer, if we take the time to relive them more gently.

• At a time of crisis, follow Christ's counsel to the sorrowing apostles: Return to Galilee! Return to the former joyful days with the Lord!

• A golden rule of Ignatius Loyola that is valid for the spiritual life is: 'Don't make a change at a time of desolation.'

Jesus in the Temple

1. Jesus in his Father's house (Lk 2:41-42): 'Now every year his parents went to Jerusalem for the festival of the Passover. And when he was twelve years old, they went up as usual for the festival.'

2. Pray Psalm 122, which people prayed on the way up to Jerusalem:
I was glad when they said to me,
'Let us go to the house of the Lord!'
Our feet are standing within your gates, O Jerusalem.

Jerusalem – built as a city that is bound firmly together.
To it the tribes go up, the tribes of the Lord,
as was decreed for Israel to give thanks to the name of the Lord.
For there the thrones for judgement were set up,
the thrones of the house of David.

Pray for the peace of Jerusalem: 'May they prosper who love you.
Peace be within your walls, and security within your towers.'
For the sake of my relatives and friends I will say, 'Peace be within you.' For the sake of the house of the Lord our God, I will seek your good.

3. See Jesus in the temple seated among the teachers, listening to them and asking them questions (Lk 2:47): 'And all who heard him were amazed at his understanding.'

4. Jesus remains in the temple (Lk 2:43 -45): 'When the festival was ended and they started to return, the boy Jesus stayed behind in Jerusalem, but his parents did not know it. Assuming that he was in the group of travellers, they went a day's journey. Then they started to look for him among their relatives and friends. When they did not find him, they returned to Jerusalem to search for him.'

5. Listen to the exchange between Jesus and his parents (Lk 2:48-49): 'When his parents saw him they were astonished; and his mother said to him, "Child, why have you treated us like this? Look, your father and I have been searching for you in great anxiety."

He said to them, "Why were you searching for me? Did you not know that I must be in my Father's house?"'
6. *The child grew (Lk 2:52):* 'And Jesus increased in wisdom and in years, and in divine and human favour.'
'Each human being is responsible for his or her own growth and advance.'

The Duck!

This is the story that the holy Sufi, named Shams-e Fabrizi, tells about himself:
'Since childhood I have been considered a mystic:
No one seemed to understand me. My father said:
"You are not suffering enough to be put in a hospice
nor are you focused enough to be sent to a monastery.
I don't know what to do with you."
I said in reply,
"They once put a duck egg under a hen.
Out of it emerged
a duck who followed its mother everywhere;
until one day the hen took it near a lakeside.
Immediately the duck went into the water
while the mother hen clucked nervously on the shore.
For I have gone into the ocean, dear father,
and it is not my fault
if you prefer to remain forever on the beach!"'

16

Contemplating the Joyful Mysteries

1. Begin with any exercise from 1 to 12.
2. After having contemplated the Joyful Mysteries, one by one, we may practise what the *Spiritual Exercises* call the application of the senses on the five previous contemplations.
3. One hour may be devoted to each 'mystery,' following this application of the senses method.
4. In learning spiritual things, the soul acts in a way that has been compared traditionally to exercising the five senses: sight, touch, hearing, smell, taste. This grasp, however, is intuitive in nature. It becomes possible only through the simplification of the spiritual faculties. Thus it is that St Ignatius proposes the 'application of the senses' in the final effort of a day as though to gather all its fruit. Such a prayer clearly is a sign of progress over discursive forms of meditation.
5. There is also a movement upward within the sequence of a single exercise. It begins with the application of sight and hearing which in the spiritual sense symbolise the opening of living faith; it then continues with smell and taste, or 'internalisation,' symbolising assimilation and the steadiness of hope; and it finally comes to its end through the communication of the person with the Living God in love.

FOCUS

• We present the rest of this exercise along the lines of St Ignatius in the *Spiritual Exercises* number 121-126.

• The symbolism at the heart underlying this language should not be a hindrance to prayer. On the contrary, it is a method of contemplation in which 'feeling present to mystery' and emotion should be pre-dominant. The point is not to weary the imagination, but to feel oneself gently present.

CONTEMPLATION

Application of the Senses

1. *Application of the senses in each of the mysteries meditated:* 'The first point is to see the persons in my imagination, contemplating and meditating in detail the circumstances surrounding them, and I will then draw some spiritual profit from this scene' *(Spiritual Exercises)*. For example, if the contemplation is about the Nativity: see Mary, Joseph, the newborn Jesus, the shepherds, the cave, the manager.

2. 'The second point is to hear what they are saying, or what they might say, and I will reflect within myself to draw some fruit from what I have heard' *(Spiritual Exercises)*. Hear Mary's tender words to Jesus. Imagine the words of Joseph, the angel, the shepherds.

3. 'The third point is to smell and taste in my imagination the infinite fragrance and sweetness of the Divinity, and of the soul, and of its virtues, and of all else, according to the character of the person I am contemplating. And I will reflect within myself to draw spiritual profit therefrom' *(Spiritual Exercises)*. In this step St Ignatius has included smell and taste. They may be contemplated separately. Feel the fragrances of the virtues of Mary and Joseph. Experience interior joy over the beauty in that scene of the birth of this child.

4. 'The fourth point is to use in imagination the sense of touch, for example by embracing and kissing the place where the persons walk or sit, always endeavouring to draw some spiritual fruit from this' *(Spiritual Exercises)*. Depending on how each person feels, one may ask Mary for the child, to kiss it, adore it. If you do not become as children, you shall not enter the kingdom of God.

There Within

The disciple asked his master for a word of wisdom.

The master answered: 'Feel as though you are inside your cell, and it alone will teach you wisdom.'

'But I don't have a cell. I'm not a monk!'

'But of course you have a cell: take a good look inside yourself!'

17

Imaginative Faith

1. This prayer hour can begin with an exercise (1 to 9) to create a climate of concentration and peace.
2. Imagine Christ seated (look at an empty chair and think that the Lord is there). Speak softly. Speaking helps make thought more explicit. For example: talk to Jesus about what is happening lately with us in our daily 'encounter' with him in prayer.
3. Also listen to what Jesus has to say. He speaks in the centre of our heart. The Father has said: 'This is my Son, my chosen one. Listen to him.'

FOCUS

• *Thought:* talk about yourself. *Prayer:* speaking with God. 'Prayer is a dialogue with the one that we know loves us' (St Teresa).

• The method that St Teresa recommends for practising during the day is to 'Keep Christ at your side.' It is the most effective way to experience Christ's presence in our life.

• If 'daily contemplation' is performed with fidelity and enthusiasm we will have to open ourselves to a 'spiritual director' who accompanies us in our journey.

CONTEMPLATION

Jesus' First Sign

1. Feel that you are present at the supper (Jn 2:1-2): Invited like Jesus to the wedding feast, Mary eagerly accepts because it is a wonderful chance to meet her son again. 'On the third day there was a wedding in Cana of Galilee, and the mother of Jesus was there. Jesus and his disciples had also been invited to the wedding.'
2. They had no wine (Jn 2:3): 'When the wine gave out, the mother of Jesus said to him, "They have no wine".'

3. *Mary knows the heart of the Son:* Whatever the meaning of Jesus' words ('Women, what concern is that to you and me? My hour has not come.') might be, it is very clear that Mary at that moment revealed that she had an unlimited faith in the power of her Son and that she knew perfectly, better than anyone, how great was Jesus' heart. Without hesitating, she ordered the servants, 'Do whatever he tells you' (5).

4. *And the miracle took place at Mary's request:* Without fanfare it was changed into superb wine, better than what had been served before. 'Now standing there were six stone water jars for the Jewish rites of purification each holding twenty or thirty gallons. Jesus said to them, "Fill the jars with water." And they filled them up to the brim. He said to them, "Now draw some out, and take it to the chief steward," so they took it. When the steward tasted the water that had become wine, and did not know where it came from (though the servants who had drawn the water knew), the steward called the bridegroom and said to him, "Everyone serves the good wine first, and then the inferior wine after the guests have become drunk. But you have kept the good wine until now"' (Jn 2:6-10).

The Star

I look at the wedding banquet of Cana
and I also go into the feast.
I see that Mary is also taking part.
I note her happiness …
And I hear the request she makes to Jesus …
I see how Jesus responds to Mary's request.
I seek some words for praising Mary,
and these come to my mind:
'Mother of mercy, life and sweetness, our hope.'

18

Symbolic Imagination

1. Do a relaxation and silence exercise, possibly number 1.
2. Identify with one of these ideas: hut on a mountain, a stream, a tree, Jacob's well, an eagle, the sea, the river, or others. Examine the roots of the choice you have made.
3. Imagine yourself as a museum statue. Imagine that it is in a dark room that is gradually being lit.
4. Imagine that this statue of ours truly reveals what we are. What should it be like?
5. Imagine Christ contemplating our statue. What does he think? How would he touch it up?

FOCUS

• This exercise can be performed in a group, each person being asked to identify with any object; and after some minutes of silence, each one presents himself or herself being the 'tree,' the 'well,' the stream,' and so forth. Each says why he or she would like to identify with that object.

• If alone, we can converse with Jesus.

CONTEMPLATION

Jesus and the Samaritan Woman

1. Feel that you are present at the dialogue of Jesus with the Samaritan woman (Jn 4:1-42). Note how the dialogue gradually changes the Samaritan woman:

• mistrustful: 'How is it that you, a Jew, ask a drink of me, a woman of Samaria?' (9);

• materialistic: 'Sir, you have no bucket, and the well is deep. Where do you get that living water?' (11);

• aggressive: 'Are you greater than our ancestor Jacob, who

gave us the well, and with his sons and flocks drank from it?' (12);

• selfish: 'Sir, give me this water, so that I may never be thirsty or have to keep coming here to draw water' (15);

• woman with five husbands, but sincere: 'I have no husband' (17);

• religiously dissatisfied: 'Our ancestors worshipped on this mountain, but you say that the place where people must worship is in Jerusalem' (20);

• she discovers that she has before her a prophet: 'Sir, I see that you are a prophet' (19); 'He told me everything I have ever done' (39);

• she believes in Jesus and becomes a missionary: 'Many Samaritans from that city believed in him because of the woman's testimony' (39);

• the terms used in succession: 'Jew' (9), 'Lord [Sir]' (11), 'greater than Jacob' (12), 'Prophet' (19), 'Messiah' (26 and 29), 'Saviour of the world' (42), show growing awareness of Jesus.

2. Pedagogy of Jesus

• He appears with human weakness: 'tired out by his journey' (6).

• He asks the Samaritan woman for water: 'Give me a drink' (7).

• In very simple language he gradually introduces her into the mystery 'of living water' (10).

• His starting point is the Samaritan woman's own life situation, 'Go, call your husband, and come back' (16).

• He is honest with the Samaritan: 'You are right in saying, "I have no husband"; for you have had five husbands, and the one you have now is not your husband. What you have said is true!' (17-18).

• He deals with the religious question in terms of what the woman says: 'Woman, believe me, the hour is coming when you will worship the Father neither on this mountain nor in Jerusalem. You worship what you do not know; we worship what we know, for salvation is from the Jews. But the hour is coming, and is now here, when the true worshippers will worship the Father in Spirit and truth, for the Father seeks such as these to worship him' (21-23).

• He presents himself as Messiah: 'I am he, the one who is speaking to you.'

• Christ turns the Samaritan into a missionary: 'Many Samaritans from that city believed in him because of the woman's testimony' (39).

3. *The water jug left behind. She is captivated by Jesus and has forgotten everything else:* 'Then the woman left her water jar and went back to the city. She said to the people, "Come and see a man who told me everything I have ever done! He cannot be the Messiah can he?"' (28-29).

The Fountain

There in the desert, near a well, on a certain day,
Jesus asked a woman for a little water,
but that sinner, speaking sarcastically,
treated him as though he were an ordinary Jew.
And he said: 'If you knew the gift that I am, woman,
it would be you who would be asking me for water
and I would not give you just ordinary water
but some that would forever slake the thirst within us ...'
And the sinner heard the words of life,
like waters that moisten the parched land
that sin had created within her ...
Then, leaving the jug and her sins at the well,
she ran to the town and exclaimed excitedly,
'Come my friends, I have found a Fountain of Love!'

19

Ignatian Contemplation

Ignatius envisions prayer as lasting an hour, 'more, rather than less'; in a time of consolation, that is easy, but it becomes difficult in desolation (*Spiritual Exercises*, 13). Ignatian prayer has the following steps:

1. *Preparatory prayer:* Ignatius begins prayer by purifying the intention and says: 'The purpose of preparatory prayer is to ask of God our Lord the grace that all my intentions, actions and works may be directed purely to the service and praise of his divine Majesty' *(Spiritual Exercises)*.

2. *Recalling the story:* It consists of a short summary of the matter to be contemplated – the story of the birth of Jesus, for example.

3. *Composition of place:* 'The image will consist of seeing with the mind's eye the physical place where that the object that we wish to contemplate is present … for instance, a temple, or mountain …' *(Spiritual Exercises)*.

4. *Petition:* 'The second prelude is to ask God our Lord for what I want and desire …Therefore, if the contemplation is on the resurrection, I shall ask for joy with Christ rejoicing …'

5. *The body of the contemplation:* It consists of seeing, listening, reflecting, judging, drawing conclusions for life in accordance with the mystery or topic meditated upon. Generally three or four points are covered.

6. *Colloquy:* At the end of the prayer, speak with God, with the Father, the Son, the Holy Spirit, with Mary, in accordance with each one's own internal rhythm. This can occur while the prayer is unfolding.

• This method, which may seem artificial, is nonetheless what we do naturally and spontaneously. It is a method that should be helpful. If it is too rigid, it may have the opposite result.

• Contemplation of the healing of the paralytic of Beth-zatha may be carried out along the lines of the method called Ignatian contemplation.

CONTEMPLATION

Healing of the Paralysed Man at Beth-zatha

1. *The healing of the paralysed man in Beth-zatha on the Sabbath day (Jn 5:1-18):* Contemplate this passage following the Ignatian method.

2. *Preparatory prayer:* Ignatius begins prayer by purifying intention. He says, 'The purpose of preparatory prayer is to ask of God our Lord the grace that all my intentions, actions, and works may be directed purely to the service and praise of his divine majesty' *(Spiritual Exercises).*

3. *Recall the story:* Jesus comes across an old man who is paralysed alongside the pool of Beth-zatha and with his power says to him: 'Stand up.' The Jews criticised the healing, because it happened on the Sabbath.

4. *Composition of place:* View the pool and such a large number of people waiting for the water to be stirred. Then view the temple, the crowd, and Jesus with the old man who has been miraculously healed.

5. *Petition:* It will be a matter of asking to get to know the Lord intimately in order to love him more and follow him.

6. *In the body of the prayer:* make yourself present to mystery.

• *First point:* See, as Jesus saw, those 'many invalids – blind, lame, and paralysed' (3) next to the pool. 'One man was there who had been ill for thirty-eight years' (5). Consider the disastrous state of this sick man who has been bearing that situation his whole life. He makes no request, shows no hope, no sign of faith – he does not even know who Jesus is. Reflect on the feelings passing through Christ's generous and sensitive heart.

• *Second point:* Listen to Jesus' exchange with the paralytic: 'When Jesus saw him lying there and knew that he had been there a long time, he said to him, "Do you want to be made well?" The sick man answered him, "Sir, I have no one to put me into the pool when the water is stirred up: and while I am making my way, someone else steps down ahead of me." Jesus said to him, "Stand up, take your mat and walk"' (Jn 5:6-8).

• Listen to the kind tone of Jesus' words ('Do you want to be made well?'), and the skeptical and desperate tone of the old, sick man telling his sad story; and the confident tone of Jesus' words ('Stand up, take your mat and walk'). Consider Jesus' feelings of compassion and joy, and the paralysed man's feelings of joy and gratitude. Consider how Jesus takes in the life of so many sick and poor people, outcasts without hope. Reflect on what should be your feelings and attitudes in relation to theirs. All are awaiting someone to plunge them into the pool when the waters are stirred. St Francis of Assisi takes Jesus down from the cross. St Anthony of Padua holds the child Jesus in his arms. St Teresa of Avila wipes the sweat from Jesus' brow in Gethsemani. And what are you doing for your outcast brother or sister?

• *Third point:* Be present at the meeting of the paralysed man with the Jews and listen to the exchange between them: 'Now that day was a Sabbath, so the Jews said to the man who had been cured, "It is the sabbath; it is not lawful for you to carry your mat." But he answered them, "The man who made me well said to me 'Take up your mat and walk'." They asked him, "Who is the man who said to you, 'Take up your mat and walk'?" (10-12). Consider the difference between the heart of Jesus and those of these Jews. They do not understand anything about kindness and compassion – for them it is law over love, structure over person. The Jews sought to curtail the joy of the poor paralysed man whom Jesus had healed. Reflect on whether your feelings of envy or selfishness blind you to your brothers and sisters. It is easier to 'accompany in feeling than to share in the joy of my brothers and sisters. There is more commitment in going to a party than in going to a funeral.'

20

Harmonising Memories

1. Go back to a memory of your past, in which there was a special experience of God. A summons, a very special call.
2. See what your response was to this call from God.
3. Relive as well as possible that moment and confirm or censure your response to Jesus crucified. Without speaking, just feeling. Christ knows your heart.

FOCUS

• St Ignatius regards 'feeling' as very important: 'For it is not an abundance of knowledge that fills and satisfies the soul but rather an interior understanding and savouring of things' *(Spiritual Exercises)*.

• The 'feeling' St Ignatius speaks about in the *Exercises* is the fruit of the Holy Spirit, who makes possible a spiritual grasp of the things of God. It is simultaneously knowledge and love. It crowns the soul inasmuch as it permits the exercise of faith on earth.

CONTEMPLATION

Calling of the Twelve

1. Jesus chooses twelve apostles (Mk 3:13-14): 'He went up the mountain and called to him those whom he wanted, and they came to him. And he appointed twelve, whom he also named apostles, to be with him, and to be sent out to proclaim the message' (13-14). Christ calls those whom he wants to be with him, and sends them on mission.

2. Conditions that Jesus imposes:

• 'They left everything and followed him' (Lk 5:11).

• 'Foxes have holes, and birds of the air have nests; but the Son of Man has nowhere to lay his head' (Mt 8:20).

• In communion of life with the Master, leaving family behind. 'Whoever comes to me and does not hate father and mother, wife and children, brothers and sisters, yes, and even life itself, cannot be my disciple' (Lk 14:26).

3. Reward:

• The kingdom: 'I confer on you … a kingdom' (Lk 22:29).

• A hundredfold and eternal life: 'And everyone who has left houses or brothers or sisters or father or mother or children or fields, for my name's sake, will receive a hundred fold, and will inherit eternal life' (Mt 19:29).

• Friendship with Christ: 'I do not call you servants any longer, because the servant does not know what the master is doing; but I have called you friends, because I have made known to you everything that I have heard from my Father' (Jn 15:15).

• 'I go to prepare a place for you' (Jn 14:3).

• 'And I will ask the Father, and he will be with you forever' (Jn 14:16).

4. Jesus appreciates the work of his disciples:

• 'You are the salt of the earth … You are the light of the world' (Mt 5:13-14).

• '… your names are written in heaven' (Lk 10:20).

• 'I thank you, Father … because you have hidden these things from the wise and the intelligent and have revealed them to infants' (Lk 10:21).

5. The apostles' response:

• 'Immediately they … followed him' (Mt 4:20).

• 'Immediately they left the boat and their father, and followed him' (Mt 4:22).

• '… they rejoiced that they were considered worthy to suffer dishonour for the sake of the name' (Acts 5:41).

21

Value of Life

1. Choose at will any exercise from 1 to 12 to relax and create silence.
2. Imagine that at a visit to the doctor you are told that you have only two months of life left.
3. How do you react? To whom will you go to tell this news?
4. Will you go to the church? Will you remain alone conversing with God until you find inner peace?
5. Do you feel the natural attachment to life? Would you like to keep on living?
6. In countless personal statements people who have been kidnapped, imprisoned, or in danger of losing their life say that under such circumstances they have learned to place importance on more serious values and have changed the way they live.
7. The best things in life are free. You only appreciate them when you are in danger of losing them. Among such things is life itself.
8. In order to draw the results hoped for from the Ignatian meditation on the Two Banners, consider that you stand at a decisive moment of life and that your option for Christ is decisive because its consequences are eternal.

FOCUS

• This contemplation is important because it disposes us to choose now what we would like to be choosing at the hour of our ultimate encounter with God.

• This is the traditional theme of the Two Cities.

• The battle between Christ and Satan takes place in the human heart.

CONTEMPLATION

The Two Banners

1. A twofold law within us: the law of the flesh and the law of the Spirit. 'So I find it to be a law that when I want to do what is good, evil lies close at hand' (Rom 7:21). '... But I see in my members another law at war with the law of my mind, making me captive to the law of sin that dwells in my members' (Rom 7:23). 'For the law of the Spirit of life in Christ Jesus has set you free from the law of sin and of death' (Rom 8:2).

2. The aims of the enemy are also opposed to those of Christ: Jesus 'went about doing good and healing all who were oppressed by the devil' (Acts 10:38).

• 'To set the mind on the flesh is death, but to set the mind on the Spirit is life and peace' (Rom 8:6).

• Jesus 'shared the same things, so that through death he might destroy the one who has the power of death, that is, the devil' (Heb 2:14).

• 'The love of the Father is not in those who love the world; for all that is in the world – the desire of the flesh, the desire of the eyes, the pride in riches – comes not from the Father but from the world' (1 Jn 2:15-16).

3. The values are likewise different (Mt 4:1-11):

• gluttony: 'If you are the Son of God, command these stones to become loaves of bread';

• ostentation: 'If you are the Son of God, throw yourself down';

• ambition for wealth: 'All these things I will give you, if you will fall down and worship me.'

• Jesus has other values (Phil 2:5-8) 'Let the same mind be in you that was in Christ Jesus, who, though he was in the form of God, did not regard equality with God as something to be exploited, but emptied himself, taking the form of a slave, being born in human likeness. And being found in human form, he humbled himself and became obedient to the point of death – even death on a cross.'

22

Discernment Examination: Movie of My Life

1. Begin this 'encounter with God' with a relaxation exercise perhaps.
2. Run the movie of your life starting in the present and going back to earliest years of which you are aware.
3. Relive the moments of your life that have left the strongest imprint.
4. Try to identify the special moments of grace.
5. See how difficulties were overcome.
6. Consider how God was involved at moments of joy as well as in hardships and suffering.

FOCUS

• God loves us as we are at this moment. View the film and accept our past with its lights and shadows.

• The past is a lesson for living the future in accordance with the will of Jesus, who loves us. The most valid experience of our past life is that God is good to us.

• In order to see whether our desires are in accordance with the designs of the Spirit and whether they are also effective, it is helpful to meditate on the three kinds of people as seen in the light of the gospel.

CONTEMPLATION

Three Types of People

1. Three kinds of People: These three kinds of people have the same problem, as St Ignatius says: 'Each of them has acquired ten thousand ducats, but not purely, as they should have, for the love of God. These men all wish to save their souls and find peace in God our Lord … ' *(Spiritual Exercises).* This is simply a hypothetical situation toward which the three kinds of people take different stances.

2. *First type:* The first type of person wants to halt disordered attachment but is unwilling to do what is necessary. Matthew's rich young man is a prototype of such people. Christ offers him the pursuit of the perfection about which he was inquiring: 'If you want to be perfect, go, sell your possessions, and give the money to the poor, and you will have treasure in heaven; then come, follow me' (21). 'When the young man heard this word, he went away grieving, for he had many possessions' (Mt 19:22).

3. *Second type:* Such people want to be freed, but without meeting the full requirements. God must go the way they want. The sons of Zebedee want to follow Jesus, but they set conditions. 'Grant us to sit, one at your right hand and one at your left, in your glory' (Mk 10:37).

4. *Third type:* This third class of people really wants to be freed of disordered affection. This is the attitude of the apostles at the very beginning: they leave everything. It is Mary's attitude: 'Here am I, the servant of the Lord; let it be done with me according to your word' (Lk 1:38).

I was sure you would come

'My buddy didn't come back from the battlefield, sir.
I'm asking for permission to go look for him.'
'Permission denied,' said the officer.
'I don't want you to risk your life for a man
who is probably dead.'
The soldier went nevertheless, and come back an hour later
mortally wounded, carrying his friend's body.
'I told you he was dead. Now I've lost both of you.
Tell me, was it worth going to bring back a dead body?'
'Oh, it was worth it, sir.
When I got there, he was still alive, and he said to me,
"Jack, I was sure you would come".'

23

Reality

1. Observe the reality of the transitory condition of human beings. With death they are deprived of the body they so love. This is a reality from which you cannot flee.
2. See the various stages of decay through which the body passes after death:
    * cold and stiffness,
    * turning blue,
    * flesh cracking,
    * decay of some parts,
    * decay of whole body,
    * barely a skeleton,
    * death of the bones,
    * dust.
3. One day, however, your body will turn glorious like that of the risen Jesus. Experience the joy and the desire of fully living this transitory life, so as to attain eternal life in heaven. 'Now if Christ is proclaimed as raised from the dead, how can some of you say there is no resurrection of the dead?' (Cor 15:12).

FOCUS

* We should be realistic and stand in the truth.
* Complete reality is life, the full life brought by Jesus.
* We have to be humble, for we shall be dust, and joyful, for we shall rise with Christ.
* The true reality is not death: complete and ultimate reality is eternal life.

CONTEMPLATION

Jesus Raises Lazarus

1. Resurrection of Lazarus (Jn 11:1-44): Feel that you are present at the supper. Jesus would not have been truly human, had he not had friends. The scene of the resurrection of Lazarus reveals with striking realism the intensity of Jesus' friendship.

2. Jesus' words and gestures 'signify' love and friendship for Lazarus. They are 'signs' that Jesus has a human heart:

* 'Jesus loved Martha and her sister and Lazarus' (5);
* 'Our friend Lazarus has fallen asleep' (11);
* Jesus 'was greatly disturbed in spirit' (33);
* 'Jesus began to weep' (35);
* 'So the Jews said, "See, how he loved him!"' (36);
* Jesus was 'again greatly disturbed' (38).

3. Martha's words and attitudes: Listen to Martha's words and observe her attitudes:

* 'Lord, he whom you love is ill' (3).
* 'She went and met him' (20).
* 'If you had been here, my brother would not have died. But even now I know that God will give you whatever you ask of him' (21-22).
* 'Yes, Lord, I believe that you are the Messiah, the Son of God, the one coming into the world' (27).

4. Mary's words and attitudes:

* 'Lord, he whom you love is ill' (3).
* 'Mary stayed at home' (20).
* 'When she heard [that the Teacher was calling for her] she got up quickly and went to him (29).... [and] knelt at his feet and said: "Lord, if you had been here, my brother would not have died"' (32).

24

EXERCISE

Awareness of the Past

1. Do a relaxation exercise, such as that of vision, number 7, in order to create a climate of silence and peace.
2. Ponder an event from the past, just one scene. Recall each gesture, each word, each glance, the reactions.
3. How did Jesus enter that scene, if he did enter it? How was it that Christ was there? He was there. Try to become aware of that.
4. He is always present in you at every moment, because he loves you! In some fashion he was seeking your 'growth' in the journey that you are making, guided by his Spirit.
5. At what moment in your life have you felt Mary's presence? What feelings and emotions did the name of Mary bring to you? Does Mary bring you peace, joy, hope?
6. At times of discouragement and hopelessness were you at peace, keeping in mind that these moments will also end and that one day the sun of hope will shine?

FOCUS

• We are finishing this second stage in which we contemplate the mysteries of Jesus' infancy and public life. Contemplation gives rise to wonder, wonder gives rise to love, and love gives rise to the desire to imitate Jesus in our lives.

• During this prayer hour, we can contemplate the path of Mary, which was also the path of Jesus, as we have seen and will see in the stages to come. This contemplation is a kind of bridge between the second and third stages.

• Mary is the best human response to the action, message, and life brought by Jesus.

CONTEMPLATION

Mary's Way of the Cross

1. The Constitution on the Church says that she 'advanced in her pilgrimage of faith.' We can see that Mary began the first stage of that pilgrimage of abnegation and cross even before Simeon told her that 'a sword will pierce your own soul' (Lk 2:35).

2. Where does God want to take me? (Lk 1:29): 'But she was much perplexed by his words and pondered what sort of greeting this might be.'

3. Alternative suffered (Mt 1:19): 'Her husband Joseph, being a righteous man and unwilling to expose her to public disgrace, planned to dismiss her quietly.'

4. Jesus has another Father (Lk 2:49-50): 'Why were you searching for me? Did you not know that I must be in my Father's house?' But they did not understand what he said to them.'

5. Jesus has a different family (Lk 11:27-28): 'While he was saying this, a woman in the crowd raised her voice and said to him, "Blessed is the womb that bore you and the breasts that nursed you!" but he said, "Blessed rather are those who hear the word of God and obey it!"'

6. She loses her Son but recovers him as head of the great body of the church (Jn 19:25-27): 'Meanwhile, standing near the cross of Jesus were his mother, and his mother's sister, Mary the wife of Clopas, and Mary Magdalene. When Jesus saw his mother and the disciple whom he loved standing beside her, he said to his mother, "Woman, here is your son." Then he said to the disciple, "Here is your mother." And from that hour the disciple took her into his own home.'

7. Mary, Mother of the Church (Acts 1:12-14): 'Then they returned to Jerusalem from the mount called Olivet, which is near Jerusalem, a Sabbath day's journey away. When they had entered the city, they went to the room upstairs where they were staying, Peter, and John, and James, and Andrew, Philip and Thomas, Bartholomew and Matthew, James son of Alphaeus, and Simon the Zealot, and Judas son of James. All these were

constantly devoting themselves to prayer, together with certain
women, including Mary the mother of Jesus, as well as his
brothers.'

God raised him up

He reduced himself to nothing,
taking on the condition of servant
and joining in solidarity with human beings.
And being regarded as a man,
he humbled himself even more,
becoming obedient even to death, and death on a cross!
That is why God has highly exalted him
and has given him a name that is above every name,
so that at the name of Jesus every knee should bend,
in heaven, on earth, and under the earth,
and every tongue proclaim, to the glory of God the Father:
'Jesus Christ is the Lord!'
– Phil 2:7-11

25

Sensitivity to People

1. Choose an exercise to produce relaxation and silence, no 7, for example.
2. Visualise the people that you are going to meet today. Visualise Christ in them. See them loved by Christ.
3. See how Christ gives himself to these persons in communion.
4. Christ took on the figure of a 'pilgrim' on the road to Emmaus, without making himself known. See that each person that you meet is Christ coming to meet us. The challenge is to recognise him, and to love him in each person.
5. Prepare to be receptive to the persons that you are to meet today.

• With this meditation on the Eucharist we enter the third stage, namely the confirmation of our love for Christ and for our brothers and sisters.

• Christ's faithful, generous, grand, and merciful love demonstrated in the Passion and in the institution of the Eucharist, should further stimulate 'my love for him' for 'he suffered all for me.'

• This series of contemplations leads to a spontaneous recognition of the love of Jesus, who suffers and dies for me. Such recognition translates into gratitude to Jesus and into love for our brothers and sisters, for Christ dies for all, and all are of equal worth in his eyes.

CONTEMPLATION

Eucharist as Communion

1. Setting in which the Last Supper is celebrated (Jn 13:1-17): All the Father's love in Jesus Christ. 'Now before the festival of the Passover, Jesus knew that his hour had come to depart from this world and go to the Father. Having loved his own who were in the world, he loved them to the end' (1).

2. With evil all around, proof of the greatest love: 'And during supper Jesus, knowing that the Father had given all things into his hands, and that he had come from God and was going to God, got up from the table, took off his outer robe, and tied a towel around himself' (2-5).

3. Example of the love that will be the bond of communion of the disciples among themselves and with Christ: 'After he had washed their feet, had put on his robe, and has returned to the table, he said to them, "Do you know what I have done to you? You call me Teacher and Lord – and you are right, for that is what I am"' (12-13).

4. Eucharist, communion among themselves and with Jesus: 'While they were eating, Jesus took a loaf of bread, and after blessing it, he broke it, gave it to the disciples, and said, "Take, eat; this is my body." Then he took a cup, and after giving thanks he gave it to them, saying, "Drink from it, all of you; for this is my blood of the covenant, which is poured out for many for the forgiveness of sins"' (Mt 26: 26-28). 'Because there is one bread, we who are many are one body, for we all partake of the one bread' (1 Cor 10:17; see also 1 Cor 11:17-34).

5. Whoever shares communion takes on the feelings of Jesus and hence the new commandment: 'I give you a new commandment, that you love one another. Just as I have loved you, you also should love one another. By this everyone will know that you are my disciples, if you have love for one another' (Jn 13:34-35).

6. The effects of communion were felt by the early Christians: 'Now the whole group of those who believed were of one heart and soul' (Acts 4:32-35).

26

EXERCISE

The Sacred Host

1. Prayer may begin with a relaxation and silence exercise, no 8, for example.
2. Imagine going into a church at night. Flickering candles light the place. Set your gaze on the white Host which stands out in the darkness at the end.
3. The Host has a power that draws your gaze and floods your whole being as if it were the centre of gravity of your life. This Host is the centre of your being and the universe.
4. The silence of that Host goes deep within you and spreads throughout the whole church. Enter into this deep silence.
5. Look once more. The Host seems to be emitting rays like a sun. These rays pour into you and purify you of selfishness, pride, ambition, indifference, hatred, and of all resentment. It seems as though after the darkness of the church, everything is now turning bright and clear. Even you yourself. Everything has become pure. Even you.
6. Now the Host is emitting energy, which brings new life and the fire of new love.
7. Now look at your heart, which seems to be changed. Rays of love are also being emitted by it, and you can share them with others. Others perceive them as Jesus can and share them, so that they may thereby be led by him through human kinship to fulfillment.
8. Open your breast and leave your own heart exposed, so that the rays coming from the Sun may warm it and produce the life of Christ in you, so that your prayer may become similar to his heart!

•The word 'Eucharist' means thanksgiving. This is just one of its many varied aspects, displaying the riches of the Eucharist.

Eucharist = supper, banquet, feast

Eucharist = viaticum, food for the journey

Eucharist = sacrifice of praise

Eucharist = sacrifice for the purification of sins

Eucharist = sacrifice of intercession to attain graces

Eucharist = Passover of the New Alliance

Eucharist = sacrifice of expiation: Christ gives himself up for us

Eucharist = communion with Christ and with our brothers and sisters

Eucharist = memorial of the Passover of the Lord

• Eucharist is celebration of the life that Jesus came to bring us.

• The Eucharist is also Passover of liberation. It celebrates the liberating initiatives of the People of God, in Jesus Christ.

CONTEMPLATION

Eucharist, Sacrifice of the New Covenant: Remembrance and Bread of Life

1. The sacrifice: The body given and blood poured out (Mt 26:26-28): 'Jesus took a loaf of bread ... and said "Take, eat; this is my body" (26). Then he took a cup, and after giving thanks he gave it to them, saying, "Drink from it, all of you; for this is my blood ... poured out for many for the forgiveness of sins"' (27).

2. Sacrifice of the New Covenant (Lk 22:20): 'This cup that is poured out for you is the new covenant in my blood.'

3. Remembrance, sacramental repetition, not mere memory (Lk22:19): 'Do this in remembrance of me.' Remembrance, sacramental repetition of the death and resurrection of Jesus, as the liturgy says.

4. The bread of life: The bread given and the blood poured out in a supper are spiritual food for our pilgrimage. Communion – Take and eat; take and drink – sustains our life. 'I am the bread of life. Your ancestors ate the manna in the wilderness, and they

died. This is the bread that comes down from heaven, so that
one may eat of it and not die. I am the living bread that came
down from heaven. Whoever eats of this bread will live forever;
and the bread that I will give for the life of the world is my flesh'
(Jn 6:48-51). 'Those who eat my flesh and drink my blood have
eternal life, and I will raise them up on the last day; for my flesh
is true food and my blood is true drink … Those who eat my
flesh and drink my blood abide in me and I in them.'

The Grain of Wheat

I was begging door to door along the village street
when your golden chariot appeared in the distance
like a marvellous dream, and I wondered who
this King of all kings might be!
My dreams swelled and I thought that
my days of woe were over.
I stood waiting for the gifts I had not asked for,
wealth pouring out on all sides.
Your chariot stopped beside me.
You looked at me and got down with a smile.
I felt that at last good fortune was entering my life.
Then, unexpectedly, you put out your hand and asked,
'Do you have something to give me?'
How noble was your gesture!
To stretch out your hand to beg of a beggar!
I stood there indecisive and confused.
Then I took out of my grain bag
the smallest grain of wheat and offered it to you.
How surprised I was at the end of the day
when I emptied my grain sack
and found a grain of gold on my poor cloth.
I wept bitterly and wished I had had the courage
to give you everything I possessed.
– R. Tagore

27

EXERCISE

Visualising the future

1. Do a relaxation and silence exercise. See number 8.
2. Also do exercise number 22, but this time begin a movie of possible future events in the present, those possible today or tomorrow. Look.
3. Observe, as though you were outside of yourself. See events as you would like them to be. Just observe them.
4. See how Christ is present in these future events.
5. How would you like him to act in future events?
6. Now strive to enter into the heart of Christ when he looked at the movie of his own future, at prayer on the night before his Passion. Be 'present to the mystery' as St Ignatius says.
7. Remain standing, near him, and listen to the prayer in which he asks the Father to deliver him from the looming drama: 'Father, if you are willing, remove this cup from me; yet, not my will but yours be done' (Lk 22:42). Note that Jesus only comes to an ultimate agreement with the Father when he seeks that solitude where an encounter with God takes place.
8. Observe how Jesus struggles with the Father and with his fate. This vision offers wisdom. Hence remain there, merely observing. His struggle with the Father continues. He perseveres in solitude for three hours. He seeks to know the Father's will and, in anguish, asks for strength to carry it out.
9. Recall similar moments of anguish in your life. How did you emerge from them? Victorious? Defeated? Other moments will come in the future. How will you prepare to face them?

• This is where contemplation on the sorrowful mysteries begins.

• In the *Spiritual Exercises*, St Ignatius is very sober in his exposition of these contemplations. If when considering the Passion of the Lord, we feel the need to multiply our reflections, it may be because we are lacking in internalisation. We need to ask for the help of the Holy Spirit so that in considering the scenes of the Passion, we may be utterly overwhelmed.

CONTEMPLATION

Jesus' Agony in the Garden

1. The supreme temptation requires special prayer (Lk 22:39-40): 'He came out and went, as was his custom, to the Mount of Olives: and the disciples followed him. When he reached the place, he said to them, "Pray that you may not come into the time of trial".'

2. Humble prayer (Mt 26:38-39): 'Then he said to them, "I am deeply grieved, even to death; remain here, and stay awake with me." And going a little farther, he threw himself on the ground and prayed, "My Father, if it is possible, let this cup pass from me; yet not what I want but what you want".'

3. Persevering prayer (Mt 26:42): 'Again he went away for the second time and prayed, "My Father, if this cannot pass unless I drink it, your will be done".'

4. Intense and desolate prayer (Lk 22:44): 'In his anguish he prayed more earnestly, and his sweat became like great drops of blood falling down on the ground.'

5. Victorious prayer (Mt 26:46): 'Get up, let us be going. See, my betrayer is at hand.'

6. Prayer urged (Lk 22:46): '… and he said to them "Why are you sleeping? Get up and pray that you may not come into the time of trial".' From beginning to end, Jesus urges his own to pray.

28

Carmelite Method

1. Begin with a relaxation and silence exercise, such as exercise no 9.

2. Among the various prayer methods or 'ways of praying,' two have become especially prominent, particularly because of the way they are organised, namely the Ignatian and the Carmelite. Both have much in common, such as a duration of one hour, in the morning or whenever it is most suited, location, position, reflection, the use of the three powers, the preference for contemplation, the dialogue with God called a colloquy. Both understand prayer to be 'an encounter of love between two persons who truly love one another: the person and God.' In her autobiography, St Teresa defines prayer as 'an intimate conversation in which the soul often speaks alone with the one by whom it knows that it is loved' (*Autobiography*, 8, 5). St Teresa highlights the affective side of prayer when she calls it 'an intimate conversation'.

3. The pattern of Carmelite prayer has seven steps:

   • *Preparation:* become aware of the presence of God or of Jesus with whom we want to converse;

   • *Reading: a lectio divina* having to do with the theme, which leads from serious reflection to commitment of the heart;

   • *Meditation and colloquy:* flowing from the reading. They are the heart of prayer and should occupy most of the time. Three books can serve as an instrument for this reading: *The Readings of the Hours,* a serious classic; *Divine Intimacy* written with a great deal of unction by Fray Gabriel de Santa Maria Magdalena; and, especially, sacred scripture.

   • *Thanksgiving, feeling, and petition:* These are the three conclusive, secondary, and spontaneous moments.

80

• What makes it difficult to do the contemplations on the Passion is that they invite us to go out from ourselves and our concerns, and from our striving to resolve those concerns.
• Two positive points in performing these contemplations is that they are a more gratuitous exercise and they open us to the suffering countenances of our brothers and sisters.

CONTEMPLATION

Jesus Is Scourged

1. The scourged body of Christ is the work of the Holy Spirit in the bosom of Mary (Lk 1:35): 'The angel said to her, "The Holy Spirit will come upon you, and the power of the Most High will over-shadow you; therefore the child to be born will be holy; he will be called Son of God".'

2. He took a human body in order to be able to suffer and die for us: 'In this is love, not that we loved God but that he loved us and sent his Son to be the atoning sacrifice for our sins' (1 Jn 4:10). 'Sacrifices and offerings you have not desired, but a body you have prepared for us' (Heb 10:5).

3. Pilate's unjust order (Jn 18:38): 'I find no case against him,' Pilate admitted, but even so, 'Pilate took Jesus and had him flogged' (Jn 19:1).

The 'Suffering Servant'

Stricken for our sins,
wounded because of our crimes.
Punishment fell upon him
for our salvation,
we were healed
by his wounds.
– Is 53:5

29

The Past and the Future

1. You may begin with a relaxation and silence exercise, no 10, for example.
2. Return to an event from the past, even if it is unimportant. Place Christ in it as a contemplation. Observe what happens.
3. Return to an event that has caused you to suffer. Make an act of faith: God willed it and was in charge over it, just as God willed and was in charge of the Passion.
4. God will draw greater good from evil: 'Oh happy fault! Oh necessary sin of Adam!'
5. Pray that you may be shown the good that God has planned to draw, or has already drawn, from that event. Praise God! – Glory to the Father – with your own words along with gestures.
6. Do the same with any foreseeable future event. Thank God in advance for the result. Ask God how you should prepare for those moments. Pray that God not be lacking in the most difficult moments in your future, and show God that you will be ready to assume with God your own part in the Passion.

FOCUS

• In these prayers, instead of reasoning, apply simple contemplation: seeing, hearing, touching, wondering, being present in the scene.

• Enter into the heart of Christ and see how he suffers out of love and without hatred.

• Strive for communion with the suffering Christ and with humankind which 'completes in its flesh what is lacking in the Passion of Christ.'

Jesus Crowned with Thorns

1. *Crowning with thorns (Mt 27:27-31):* Strive to feel present at this scene of cruel mockery: 'They stripped him and put a scarlet robe on him' (28).

2. *He is patient and silent:* '… and after twisting some thorns into a crown, they put it on his head. They put a reed in his right hand and knelt before him and mocked him, saying, "Hail King of the Jews!"' (29).

3. *With Ignatius Loyola we can ask ourselves:* And me? What have I done for Christ? What am I doing for Christ? What should I do for Christ?

4. *Jesus endures contempt:* 'They spat upon him, and took the reed and stuck him on the head' (30). And in his heart he prays to the father: 'Father, forgive them: for they do not know what they are doing' (Lk 23:34).

The 'Suffering Servant'

Despised and rejected
by humans,
a man of sorrow,
acquainted with suffering,
like one before whom
people shun their face,
despised and ignored,
yet he endured our sufferings
and bore our sorrows.
– Is 53:3-4

30

Benedictine Method

1. Begin with a relaxation and silence exercise.
2. In this prayer hour, what is known as the Benedictine method may be applied. The distinguished feature of its spirituality is a great appreciation for the divine office, which is called the 'work of God'. Monastic personal prayer is the continuation of the office. This prayer, which is called '*Lectio divina*' draws its inspiration from scripture read, meditated, and pondered, in intimacy with the Lord. It is made up primarily of three activities: reading of scripture, meditation, contemplation.
3. Reading of a scripture text (for example a psalm or a gospel passage).
4. Meditation or reflection in silence, if you are alone. If you are in a prayer group, after the reading of the text, or a portion of the text (a verse), leave a time for reflection and then comment on its fruit.
5. Leave some further time in silence for contemplation and colloquy.

• 'Contemplation' is a higher level of prayer than 'meditation' because it entails greater intimacy and union with God.
• Contemplation is a kind of prayer that is more affective and intuitive than rational, closer to silence and to the heart, to identification than to speculation, to feeling than to reason.
• To contemplate is to make yourself present at the scene, to participate, see, hear, touch, taste …
• Because it includes a number of scenes, contemplation of the Way of the Cross lends itself to this kind of method.

CONTEMPLATION

The Road to Calvary

1. *Here is the man!:* 'So Jesus came out, wearing the crown of thorns and the purple robe. Pilate said to them, "Here is the man!"' (Jn 19:5).

2. *On the cross he makes known the full extent of his love.* 'Then he handed him over to them to be crucified' (Jn 19:16).

3. *He is the 'suffering servant':* 'All we like sheep have gone astray; we have all turned to our own way, and the Lord has laid on him the iniquity of us all' (Is 53:6-7).

4. *He goes out of the city to give himself to the world:* 'So they took Jesus; and carrying the cross by himself, he went out to what is called The Place of Skull, which in Hebrew is called Golgotha' (Jn 19:17). 'And I, when I am lifted up from the earth, will draw all people to myself' (Jn 12:32).

5. *He is humble and accepts help from a creature:* 'And as they led him away, they seized a man, Simon of Cyrene, who was coming from the country, and they laid the cross on him, and made him carry it behind Jesus' (Lk 23:26).

6. *In his suffering he thinks of others:* 'A great number of the people followed him, and among them were women who were beating their breasts and wailing for him. But Jesus turned to them and said, "Daughters of Jerusalem, do not weep for me, but weep for yourselves and for your children"' (Lk 23:27-28).

31

Intensifying Silence by Song

1. Do a relaxation exercise, no 9, for example.
2. A deep silence is required to energise this contemplation on the death of Jesus on the cross. One method of attaining an intense silence is to mentally intone a short phrase, such as the *Kyrie eleison* or another short prayer. Group prayer may be sung.
3. During the prayer, repeat the same exercise to intensify the silence. This silence that the singing produces in your heart is more important than the meaning of the words.

FOCUS

• We are not going to learn anything new here, but are deepening what we receive through a concrete faith in the person of Jesus Christ.

• When we read the writings of the saints, we see that they kept coming back every day to the contemplation of the Passion of the Lord. For them the Passion of the Lord was a confirmation and a light. In it they found light!

CONTEMPLATION

Jesus Dies on the Cross

1. In the death of Christ the Father tells us of his love (Rom 5:8): 'But God proves his love for us in that while we still were sinners Christ died for us.'

2. Pray with Psalm 22: Christ prayed this psalm on the cross. In a prophetic vision, the psalmist describes the sufferings of the Messiah in which verses 7, 8, 16 and 18 are completely fulfilled, according to the explicit testimony of the evangelists. 'All who see me mock at me; they make mouths at me, they shake their heads' (7): 'Let him rescue the one in whom he delights!' (8); 'For dogs are all around me; a company of evildoers encircles me' (16); 'They divide my clothes among themselves, and for my clothing they cast lots' (18)

3. *Before surrendering his life for us, Jesus gave us the great gift of his Mother so she might be our Mother (Jn 19:25-27):* 'Meanwhile, standing near the cross of Jesus were his mother, and his mother's sister, Mary the wife of Clopas, and Mary Magdalene. When Jesus saw his mother and the disciple whom he loved standing beside her, he said to his mother, "Woman, here is your son." Then he said to the disciple, "Here is your mother." And from that hour the disciple took her into his own home.'

4. *Jesus dies on the cross (Jn 19:28-30):* 'After this, when Jesus knew that all was now finished, he said (in order to fulfill the scripture), "I am thirsty." A jar full of sour wine was standing there. So they put a sponge full of the wine on a branch of hyssop and held it to his mouth. When Jesus had received the wine, he said, "It is finished." Then he bowed his head and gave up his spirit.'

5. *Christ is victorious, and so are we with Christ (1 Cor 15:54-57):* 'When this perishable body puts on imperishability, and this mortal body puts on immortality, then the saying that is written will be fulfilled: "Death has been swallowed up on victory." "Where, O death, is your victory? Where, O death, is your sting?" The sting of death is sin, and the power of sin is the law. But thanks be to God, who gives us the victory through our Lord Jesus Christ.'

6. *The veil is torn. Pagans also have access to Jesus (Mk 15:39):* 'Truly, this man was God's Son!'

32

EXERCISE

The Name of Jesus

1. Repeat exercise no 10.
2. Invoke the Holy Spirit, without whose hope the name of Jesus cannot be properly pronounced.
3. Imagine Jesus risen or enthroned within your heart.
4. Pronounce the name of Jesus with different attitudes or feelings – adoration, love, trust, surrender, desire, repentance.
5. Listen to Jesus pronounce your name.
6. What do you experience when you hear your name coming from Jesus' lips? Detect how you feel.

FOCUS

• The purpose of contemplation on the mysteries of the resurrection is to produce within us spiritual joy which is the fruit of all contemplation. It is the special grace to be attained in this stage.
• Joy is a fruit of the Holy Spirit, the Consoler.

CONTEMPLATION

Appearance to Mary Magdalene

1. Jesus pronounces the name of Mary (Jn 20:11-18):
Reflect on the verses that touch us most within, such as:
• 'But Mary stood weeping outside the tomb' (11);
• 'Woman, why are you weeping? Whom are you looking for?' (15);
• 'Jesus said to her, "Mary!"' (16);
• The shepherd 'calls his own sheep by name' (Jn 10:3);
• 'She said to him ..."Master"' (16);
• 'Mary Magdalene went and announced to the disciples, "I have seen the Lord"' (18);
• Mary is sent by Jesus, 'But go to my brothers and say to them ...' (17).

2. There is another Mary, the Mother of Jesus, who naturally by this time has already received the first and ineffable visit from Jesus. The gospel does not tell us about it, says St Ignatius Loyola, because 'it assumes that we know about it' *(Spiritual Exercises)*. What must Mary have said? The *Magnificat* should now be intoned.

Oh Death, where is your victory?

I am going to tell you a mystery.
We will not all die
but all will be transformed,
in an instant,
in the twinkling if an eye,
at the sound of the last trumpet.
For the trumpet will sound,
and the dead will arise incorruptible
and as for us,
we should be transformed.
For indeed this perishable being
must put on imperishability,
and this mortal being
must be clothed in immortality.
Therefore when
this perishable being
shall have put on imperishability
and this mortal being
shall have put on immortality
then shall the words of scripture be fulfilled:
'Death has been swallowed up in victory.
Oh death, where is your victory?
Death, where is your sting?'
– 1 Cor 15:51-55

33

The Thousand Names of Jesus

1. A relaxation and silence exercise, such as nos 1 to 12, may be performed.
2. Repeat the previous exercise. Say the name of Jesus as many times as you find spiritual delight, with feelings of adoration, love, trust, surrender, desire, repentance.
3. Give new names to Jesus each time you inhale. Look at the psalmists' creativity: 'my rock,' 'my shield,' 'my song.' Thus: 'Jesus, my life,' 'Jesus, my joy,' 'Jesus, my strength,' 'Jesus, my love,' 'Jesus, meaning of my life,' 'Jesus, my friend,' 'Jesus, my master,' 'Jesus, Good Shepherd,' and others that appear in the New Testament.
4. Imagine that Jesus repeats these same names for you! How do you feel?

FOCUS

• St Ignatius suggests a favourable climate for this series of contemplation: 'After arousing before me the contemplation that I am going to do, desiring to be moved and joyful with such joy and happiness from our Lord Jesus Christ.'

• 'I will go in with thoughts of pleasure, happiness, and spiritual joy, as for example over the glory of heaven' (*Spiritual Exercise*).

CONTEMPLATION

They Were Filled with Joy

1. *Appearance of Jesus to the disciples (Jn 20:19-29):* Be present to the scene, that is, be inside the room with the doors closed: '...and the doors of the house where the disciples had met were locked for fear of the Jews' (19).

2. *See Jesus entering:* 'Jesus came and stood among them ...' (19).

3. Hear the words and the tone in which he says: 'Peace be with you' (19). In coming into contact with creatures, God is not like us. God greets the creature, and desires that it may have peace, which is a gift of the Holy Spirit.

4. See how he shows them the wounds in his hands and his side: '... he showed them his hands and his side' (20); 'Then the disciples rejoiced when they saw the Lord' (20).

5. Pentecost without extraordinary phenomena. Listen to the words: 'Peace be with you' (19); 'As the Father has sent me, so I send you' (21). 'Receive the Holy Spirit. If you forgive the sins of any, they are forgiven them' (22-23); this is the first ecclesial witness and the proclamation of the resurrection, which means that the Lord is present in the community.

6. Thomas goes from seeing to believing. Hear the words to Thomas: 'Then he said to Thomas, "Put your finger here and see my hands. Reach out your hand and put it in my side. Do not doubt but believe"'(27).

7. 'Thomas said, "My Lord and my God!"' (28).

8. The bold statement in St John's prologue, 'And the Word was God' becomes the expression of faith of the unbelieving Thomas: 'My Lord and my God!' Between the prologue and this epilogue lies the entire life of Jesus-Emmanuel.

9. Application of the senses:

• Take note of how often the verb 'to see' is used in this passage, of the lively dialogue, 'hearing,' and of the proof demanded by Thomas: 'touching.'

• Application of the senses of sight, hearing, and touch. Ask Jesus to allow you to kiss his wounds!

• Reflect on how we bring one another this news: 'I have seen Jesus risen.'

34

See How He Looks at You

1. You may begin with a relaxation and silence exercise.
2. In this encounter with the risen Jesus, follow the method that St Thérèse of Lisieux recommends: 'Look at him who is looking at you.' See Jesus looking at you: loving you, humbly.
3. Let him tell you of his love. There is a great deal of difference between saying, 'God loves me,' and feeling and experiencing that God tells you personally: 'So-and-so, I love you.' If it is really difficult to love, it is even harder to let yourself be loved. Ask this question honestly, 'Do I let myself be loved?'
4. Finally state your love for Jesus Christ with words, and with gestures, if you are alone.

FOCUS

• The primary fruit of these contemplations is growth in love for Jesus Christ.

• After so many contemplations, we certainly feel that we can respond very differently from the way we previously would answer the question 'Who do you say that I am?'

CONTEMPLATION

They Recognised him in the Breaking of the Bread

1. The two disciples from Emmaus (Lk 24:13-35): '… two of them were going to a village called Emmaus' (13).

2. They were talking among themselves, but not with God: '… and talking with each other about all these things that had happened' (14).

3. Jesus comes forth to meet them: 'While they were talking and discussing, Jesus himself came near and went with them …' (15).

'And he said to them, "What are you discussing with each other while you walk along?"' (17).

4. *Cleopas and his companion are the personification of despair:* 'They stood still looking sad.' 'We had hoped ... some woman ... some of those who were with us went to the tomb and found it just as the women had said, but they did not see him' (17-24).

5. *The Resurrection gives the scriptures meaning:* 'Then he said to them, "Oh, how foolish you are, and how slow of heart to believe all that the prophets have declared! Was it not necessary that the Messiah should suffer these things and then enter into his glory?" Then beginning with Moses and all the prophets, he interpreted to them the things about himself in all the scriptures' (25-27).

6. *Jesus has now won them over:* 'but they urged him strongly saying, "Stay with us, because it is almost evening and the day is now nearly over." So he went in to stay with them' (29).

7. *They recognised Jesus by his special way of breaking bread:* 'When he was at the table with them, he took bread, blessed and broke it, and gave it to them. Then their eyes were opened and they recognised him; and he vanished from their sight' (30-31).

8. *The presence of Jesus sets their hearts on fire:* 'They said to each other, "Were not our hearts burning within us while he was talking to us on the road, while he was opening the scriptures to us?' (32).

9. *Upon returning to Jerusalem, they found the Eleven and their companions gathered together and were told:* 'The Lord has risen indeed, and he has appeared to Simon!' Then they told what had happened on the road, and how he had been made known to them in the breaking of the bread' (34-35).

35

The Sea

1. Do a relaxation and silence exercise, such as no 2.
2. The Sea of Tiberias is the ideal place to spend the morning of a resurrection day. Someone has called this place a 'temple of Jesus' – a natural temple not built by anyone, one often visited by Jesus, and which witnessed miracles in the way of healings, miraculous catches of fish, storms calmed, and the scene where the first pope was chosen.
3. Jesus wanted to spend a spring morning there with seven of his disciples. Today you are invited to 'see,' 'hear,' 'contemplate,' 'reflect' at this spot where visitors today feel the presence of the resurrection in a special way.
4. Comparing the sea with the resurrection; the sea is beautiful: Contemplate the beauty of the sea. Contemplate the beauty of the resurrection. There is nothing more beautiful than a new and glorious life springing from death on the cross. The crueller and more humiliating the death, the more glorious and radiant the new life of the risen Jesus!
5. The sea is deep: Wonder at the mysteries that the sea keeps within it. So many forms of life manifest themselves in the ocean depths. The riches contained in the resurrection are also fascinating. The resurrection is more than simply returning to the previous life. It is complete, full, glorious, radiant life, that no eye has seen, nor ear has heard, nor human intelligence may comprehend …
6. The sea is vast: View horizons unveiled before our ecstatic gaze. Blue horizon on a spring morning. An Easter morning. Consider that the resurrection of Jesus is not of Jesus alone. It has an impact on the whole world, it reaches all human beings of all races, all beliefs, of all ages of history … It spreads through the entire creation for 'We know that the whole creation has been groaning …[and] we

ourselves … groan inwardly while we wait for adoption, the redemption of our bodies … and those whom he justified he also glorified' (Rom 8:22-23).

7. Just as the sea ecologically balances nature, so the resurrection puts everything in its proper order:
   • it explains the life and death of Jesus, his teachings, his words, his promises;
   • it confirms that the kingdom as instituted by Jesus is entirely meaningful;
   • that our life journey alongside Jesus is the only thing that can give our life meaning. Whoever journeys with him will be victorious!

8. The sea is in constant motion: sometimes more, sometimes less agitated, the sea is ever in motion. The ocean waves arrive meekly on the shore, one after another, or break furiously against the rocks. The effects of the resurrection are like the ocean waves: continually being produced and renewed. You can discover them on all sides:
   • in all successful liberation efforts of oppressed slaves;
   • on the faces of the sick who despite their sufferings, continue to hope;
   • in all humanitarian conquests attained by humankind to make life more just, happier, and more joyful;
   • in the happiness of the nun who radiates the joy of a fulfilled person because she has surrendered to the risen Jesus;
   • in the glorious scars proudly displayed by those who have struggled for the cause of justice.

9. You do not tire of seeing and hearing the ocean waves. They are like the merciful grace of the risen Jesus, who keeps coming back to your beach, which continually needs to be purified.

FOCUS

• This contemplation may be done over several days or a whole week.
• Allow Jesus to ask you the same question he asked Peter.

CONTEMPLATION
On the Shore of the Sea of Tiberias

1. Peter's invitation to his companions (Jn 21:1-14): 'Simon said to them, "I am going fishing"' (3). It is not like Peter to stand around with his arms folded.

2. Response of his companions: 'They said to him, "We will go with you." They went out and got into the boat, but that night they caught nothing' (3).

3. With Jesus there, things are different: 'Just after daybreak, Jesus stood on the beach; but the disciples did not know that it was Jesus. Jesus said to them, "Children, you have no fish, have you?" They answered him, "No." He said to them, "Cast the net to the right side of the boat, and you will find some," so they cast it, and now they were not able to haul it in because there were so many fish' (4-6).

4. Peter and John act in their own way: 'That disciple whom Jesus loved said to Peter, "It is the Lord!" When Simon Peter heard that it was the Lord, he put on some clothes, for he was naked, and jumped into the sea.'

5. The others remain anonymous: 'But the other disciples came in the boat, dragging the net full of fish, for they were not far from the land, only about a hundred yards off' (8).

6. Jesus is as one who serves: 'Jesus came and took the bread and gave it to them, and did the same with the fish' (13)

He is now in our house

A certain preacher always used to say:
'We have to put God in our lives!'
But in response the master said to him,
'The Lord God is already in our lives,
our job is simply to recognise him.'

36

EXERCISE

The Heart of Christ

1. Begin with a relaxation and silence exercise, such as no 2.
2. Imagine that the Risen Christ is present.
3. Christ lets you see his heart through the door of his opened side. There lies the source of everything. You receive from Jesus primarily the gift of the Spirit, symbolised by water (Jn 7:37-39), and the gift of the Eucharist, symbolised by blood (Jn 6:54-56). For there are three that testify: the Spirit, the water, and the blood (1 Jn 5:6).
4. Jesus displays his heart to tell you how much he loves you, as you are here and now, with an unconditional love. He does not know how to love 70 or 80 percent – he only knows how to love 100 percent.

FOCUS

• The core idea of the whole gospel of John is that the historic deeds of Jesus are signs by which faith discovers the deep reality of Christ and the gifts that he brings to the world.

• John's instance in telling what he, true witness, has seen, that a soldier 'pierced his side with a spear, and at once blood and water came out' (Jn 19:34), highlights not only the truth of the event, but it actually reveals what the water and the blood mean: the gift of the spirit and the gift of the Eucharist.

CONTEMPLATION

Come Holy Spirit

1. *The Holy Spirit, gift of Jesus:* 'And I will ask the Father, and he will give you another Advocate, to be with you forever' (Jn 14:16). 'When the Advocate comes, whom I will send to you from the Father, the Spirit of Truth who comes from the Father, he will testify on my behalf' (Jn 15:26).

2. The Spirit leads to the truth: 'When the Spirit of Truth comes, he will guide you into all the truth' (Jn 16:13).

3. The Spirit liberates: 'For the law of the Spirit of life in Christ Jesus has set you free from the law of sin and of death' (Rom 8:2). 'For all who are led by the Spirit of God are children of God' (Rom 8:14).

4. The Spirit gives life and peace: 'To set the mind on the Spirit is life and peace ... if by the Spirit you put to death the deeds of the body you will live' (Rom 8:6, 13).

5. The Spirit intercedes for us: 'Likewise the Spirit helps us in our weakness: for we do not know how to pray as we ought, but that very Spirit intercedes with sighs too deep for words' (Rom 8:26).

6. The Spirit dwells in us: 'Do you not know that you are God's temple and that God's Spirit dwells in you?' (1 Cor 3:16).

7. The Spirit makes us children of God: 'For all who are led by the Spirit of God are children of God. For you did not receive a spirit of Slavery to fall back into fear, but you have received a Spirit of adoption. When we cry, 'Abba! Father!' it is that very Spirit bearing witness ...' (Rom 8:14-15).

8. The Spirit's gifts are distributed: 'Now there are varieties of gifts, but the same Spirit; and there are varieties of services, but the same Lord; and there are varieties of activities, but it is the same God who activates all of them in everyone. To each is given the manifestation of the Spirit for the common good. To one is given through the Spirit the utterance of wisdom, and to another the utterance of knowledge according to the same Spirit, to another faith by the same Spirit, to another gifts of healing by the one Spirit, to another the working of miracles, to another prophecy, to another the discernment of spirits, to another various kinds of tongues, to another the interpretation of tongues. All these are activated by one and the same Spirit, who allots to each one individually just as the Spirit chooses' (1 Cor 12:4-11).

37

Intercession

1. Begin with a relaxation and silence exercise, such as 3.
2. Put yourself in contact with Christ. Imagine yourself flooded with his light, life, and power.
3. Imagine yourself laying your hands on the heads of the persons you love. Jesus dwells in each one. Ask that the love of Christ descend upon them. Wordlessly. See them illuminated by the light and love of Christ. See them transformed.
4. If weariness comes on, return to the comforting presence of Christ and rest in him for some moments. When you are refreshed return to laying your hands on them.
5. Do the same with each person with whom you have some relationship: persons entrusted to your care, family members, those with whom you live or work, persons for whom you have the greatest obligation to pray and intercede.
6. Pray for your friends, for those whom you do not like, for those who do not like you. Christ's power passes through your hands to each of these persons.
7. Pray for whole nations, for those that have greater responsibilities and power, for the poorer ones, for those who are at war …
8. Leave your mind blank for a few moments, and ask the Holy Spirit to suggest to you persons for whom or intentions for which you ought to pray. Pour the treasures of Christ over others, for they are infinite. The more you share with others, the more will you nourish your own heart.
9. Bring to your mind persons you know who are going through a crisis of discouragement and lay your hands on them, asking God to enlighten and aid them in such moments.

• The importance of intercession in St Ignatius (*Constitutions*, part 10). St Francis Xavier, Curé d'Ars, St Paul. The vision that Teilhard de Chardin had of the nun at prayer.

• This way of praying is recommended and practised by Jesus. It is the work of Jesus today, always interceding for us. He 'always lives to make intercession' for us (Heb 7:25). The 'very Spirit intercedes for us with sighs too deep for words' (Rom 8:26). Mary intercedes for us as she did at the wedding feast of Cana.

CONTEMPLATION

The New Commandment

1. *The new commandment (Jn 13:34):* 'I give you a new commandment, that you love one another. Just as I have loved you, you also should love one another.'

2. *This is the true witness of Christ (Jn 13:35):* 'By this everyone will know that you are my disciples, if you have love for one another.'

3. *Love above all (1 Cor 13:1-3):* 'If I speak in the tongues of mortals and of angels, but do not have love, I am a noisy gong or a clanging cymbal. And if I have prophetic powers, and understand all mysteries and all knowledge, and if I have all faith, so as to remove mountains, but do not have love, I am nothing. If I give away all my possessions, and if I hand over my body so that I may boast, but do not have love, I gain nothing.'

4. *Characteristics of love (1Cor 13:4-7):* 'Love is patient; love is kind; love is not envious or boastful or arrogant or rude. It does not insist on its own way; it is not irritable or resentful; it does not rejoice in wrongdoing, but rejoices in the truth. It bears all things, believes all things, hopes all things, endures all things.'

5. *Love never ends (1 Cor 13:8,13):* 'Love never ends … And now faith, hope, and love abide, these three; and the greatest of these is love.'

Love is Eternal

Love will never end.
But as for prophecies, they will end,
tongues will cease,
knowledge will disappear.
For our knowledge is imperfect,
and so is our prophecy.
But when that which is perfect arrives,
that which is imperfect will disappear.
Thus, when I was a child,
I spoke like a child,
I felt like a child,
I thought like a child;
but when I became an adult
I left the things of a child behind.
Now we see in a mirror, and things are blurry,
but then it will be face to face.
Now I know imperfectly,
but then I shall know as I am known.
Now there remain these three things,
faith, hope, and love;
but the greatest of them is love.
– *1 Cor 13:8-13*

38

The Name As Presence

1. Begin with a relaxation exercise, such as no 4.
2. The name indicates presence: meditate on Mary's presence in your life. Feel that Mary's presence is growing in your heart. How? What feelings do you detect in your heart when you pronounce the name of Mary? What other words can you combine with Mary? 'Mother of Christ?' 'My Mother?' Others? The church has fashioned a litany. Make your own.
3. Feel now how his name beats in the heart of the saints. How do others see the presence of Mary? With what aspirations, what feelings? Why are her shrines so visited?
4. Strive to enter once more into the heart of the Son and see what he feels for Mary. Admiration? Gratitude? Affection? What did Jesus do and what would he still like to do for her?
5. Strive to grasp the emotions that this name arouses in the hearts of those who love Mary.
6. Go back to detecting the emotions that the name of Mary is stirring at this moment.

CONTEMPLATION

Rejoice, Mary, Full of Grace

1. Slowly pray the Hail Mary.

2. 'Hail Mary, full of grace' (Lk 1:28): The better translations of the bible render this as 'Rejoice, you who have favour with God, the Lord is with you.' It is not the simple Greek greeting, 'Be well,' or the Latin 'Ave' that appears so often in the classics as a greeting, 'Ave Caesar,' but an invitation to joy: 'Rejoice' (*chaire* in Greek).

3. 'The Lord is with you' (Lk 1:28): Besides being a portent, these words added by the angel are a divine guarantee for the new and great commitment that Mary is to assume: to be the mother of Jesus.

4. *Luke says, 'The virgin's name was Mary' (Lk 1:27):* This is the first time that the name of Mary appears given to Our Lady. The last time that the New Testament refers to Mary by this name is Acts 1:14: 'All these were constantly devoting themselves to prayer, together with certain women, including Mary the mother of Jesus.' Mary (Greek and Latin) corresponds to the Hebrew Miriam. It is a name used rather often in the New Testament: Mary, mother of James and John, Mary Magdalene, Mary sister of Martha, Mary mother of Mark, and another Mary in Rom 16:6.

5. *'Blessed art thou amongst women and blessed is the fruit of your womb' (Lk 1:42):* Mary is greeted as happy among all women for the child that she will bear is blessed and is the Lord. 'And why has this happened to me, that the mother of my Lord comes to me?' (Lk 1:43).

6. *Holy Mary, Mother of God:* this second part of the Hail Mary comes from the church. In it, after praising Mary for being mother of God, with sinners we plead for protection at this moment and at the moment of our departure, at the hour of our death.

7. *Holy Mary:* Mary is holy because she is full of grace and because the mission for which she has been chosen is the holiest that a human can have: 'being the Mother of God.'

8. *Mother of God:* The divine election by which Mary is chosen to be mother of the Word Incarnate confers on Mary the greatest dignity to which a human creature can be raised and it is the source of all the other privileges attributed to her: 'virginity,' 'being conceived without sin,' 'being Mother of the Church,' 'having been elevated in body and soul to heaven,' and so forth.

9. *Pray for us sinners, now and at the hour of our death:* We appeal to Mary because she is both mother of Jesus and our mother, and it attests to the fact that the Christian people are devoted to her as intercessor along with her Son Jesus.

10. We may use the same method to contemplate the *Magnificat*, litany, and *Salve Regina*.

39

The Name As Salvation

1. Begin with a silence and relaxation exercise, such as no 5.
2. The name of Jesus brings saving presence: Jesus means Saviour: 'There is salvation in no one else' (Acts 4:12). His name uttered with love brings forgiveness.
3. The name of Jesus as remedy heals the entire person. 'Fear is lost, any illness is cured by means of the name of God alone!' (Mahatma Gandhi). Remedy of the poor.
4. Receive the name gently, desiring to be invaded by the presence of Jesus.
5. Perform the anointing of the senses and faculties with this name: 'Your name is perfume poured out' (Song 1:3): eyes, ears, lips, tongue, hands, feet …memory, mind, will, imagination, heart, emotional life. See each sense, member, faculty inundated with the presence and power of Jesus.
6. Pour this anointing over each one of the persons for whom you wish to pray: the ill, those who suffer, friends, your enemies. See each person illuminated by the power of Jesus.

FOCUS

• For Semites, the name (shêm) is not something empty, but something powerful that makes a person really present (1 Sam 25:25).

• The name of Yahweh is protection and refuge (Prov 18:10).

• The name expresses the greatness, fame, and glory of its bearer through whose intervention something is expected and should happen.

• The name expresses the function of the one who bears it, his or her calling and reason for being.

• Often in the bible the name stands for the person, and hence some bibles replace 'name' with 'person': 'name of Jesus' is rendered 'person of Jesus'.

CONTEMPLATION

The Holy Name of Jesus

1. The name of Jesus as Saviour (Mt 1:21): 'She will bear a son, and you are to name him Jesus, for he will save his people from their sins.' 'But you were washed, you were sanctified, you were justified in the name of the Lord Jesus Christ and in the Spirit of our God' (1 Cor 6:11). '... there is no other name under heaven given among mortals by which we must be saved' (Acts 4:12).

2. The name of Jesus as power and strength (Acts 3:6): 'But Peter said, "I have no silver or gold, but what have I give you; in the name of Jesus Christ of Nazareth, stand up and walk." And by faith in his name, his name itself has made this man strong, whom you see and know; and the faith that is through Jesus has given him this perfect health in the presence of all of you' (Acts 3:16).

3. The name of Jesus, hope and protection (Mt 12:21): 'In his name the Gentiles will hope.' 'Very truly, I tell you, if you ask anything of the Father in my name, he will give it to you' (Jn 16:23).

4. Greatness and glory of the name of Jesus (Phil 2:9-11): 'Therefore God also highly exalted him and gave him the name that is above every name, so that at the name of Jesus every knee should bend, in heaven and on earth and under the earth, and every tongue should confess that Jesus Christ is Lord, to the glory of God the Father.'

5. The disciples announced the name of Jesus (Acts 9:15): 'But the Lord said to him, "Go, for he is an instrument whom I have chosen to bring my name before Gentiles and kings and before the people of Israel."' Saul 'went in and out among them in Jerusalem, speaking boldly in the name of the Lord' (Acts 9:28).

6. The greatest gift that has been given us in the name of Jesus (Jn 14:26). 'But the Advocate, the Holy Spirit, whom the Father will send in my name, will teach you everything, and remind you of all that I have said to you.'

Remember the Leader!

A story by Nathaniel Hawthorne
tells of a giant face carved into a rock
standing over a broad valley.
A tradition said
that the leader for the people who lived there
would arise one day
and that the leader would have the features
of that powerful and mighty face
represented in the sculpture.
And one day the hero arose.
From pondering and admiring the sculpture so much,
young Earnest gradually took on
the features of the sculpture,
and as a young man
he gradually forged in himself the character
and spirit of a genuine leader,
who as an adult freed his people.
Better yet,
contemplation of the ideal
represented in the sculpture,
awakened the leader lying dormant in Earnest's heart.
And Christ said:
'I am the way.
Learn from me!'

40

Praying with Holy Desire

1. Begin with a relaxation and silence exercise, such as no 5.
2. Pray with holy desire. Begin the prayer by joining in solidarity with your brothers and sisters. It is not necessary to say a formal prayer. Simply present to God your desires for others: family members, friends, community, the church, the world. In his prayer St Ignatius Loyola often expressed his desire by wanting to be like the saints: 'St Dominic, St Francis did such and such: I should try to do more!' St Teresa used to say: 'Strive to go about with joy and freedom … have confidence … encourage yourself to do great things … His majesty wants lively souls' (*Life of St Teresa*, 13:1-3).
3. Psychologically you cannot attain what you do not even desire! Normally your desires go further and soar higher than your activity, but even so, God rejoices in your good intentions.
4. An intention may be equivalent to an act of contrition that purifies you of your sins; it can be an act of love that merits you God's graces.
5. 'Every desire for God to come to us is already prayer. There is an inner prayer that never ceases – your desire. If you desire to pray without ceasing, never cease desiring' (St Augustine).
6. Your desires reveal who you are. God knows your desires and judges you by the deepest desires that exist in your heart, even while knowing that in practice, many of them will not be achieved because of your weakness. You must continually evaluate your desires to see whether they proceed from the Holy Spirit dwelling within you.

FOCUS

• ' … love consists in a mutual interchange by the two parties, that is to say, that the lover gives to and shares with the beloved all that he has or can attain, and that the beloved acts toward the lover in like manner. Thus if one has knowledge, one shares it with the one who does not have it. In like manner they share honours, riches, and all things' *(Spiritual Exercises)*.

• Each of the next four contemplations expresses the law of communication by which St Ignatius defined love: All comes from God and all must be offered to God in return.

• This is a way of praying for someone who knows how to find love for God in all things.

• Love is a grace obtained from God through prayer, not the result of human effort.

CONTEMPLATION TO ATTAIN LOVE
What the Father Gives Us in Christ

1. The gift of the Father (1 Jn 4:8-9):
'Whoever does not love does not know God, for God is love. God's love was revealed among us in this way: God sent his only Son into the world so that we might live through him.'
'For God so loved the world that he gave his only Son, so that everyone who believes in him may not perish but may have eternal life' (Jn 3:16).
2. The gifts of creation in Christ (Jn 1:3):
'All things came into being through him, and without him not one thing came into being.'
'He who did not withhold his own Son, but gave him up for all of us, will he not with him also give us everything else?' (Rom 8:32).
3. In him we have life (Jn 10:10):
'I came that they may have life, and have it abundantly.'
'I am the bread of life. Whoever comes to me will never be hungry, and whoever believes in me will never be thirsty' (Jn 6:35). 'I am the living bread that came down from heaven. Whoever eats of this bread will live forever' (Jn 6:51).

4. He is our peace and brings about union (Eph 2:14):
'For he is our peace; in his flesh he has made both groups into one.'
' ... to gather up all things in him, things in heaven and things on earth' (Eph 1:10).

5. In him we are children of God (Eph 1:5): 'He destined us for adoption as his children through Jesus Christ ...'

6. The gift of the Holy Spirit has come to us through Christ (Eph 1:13): 'In him you ... were marked with the seal of the promised Holy Spirit.'

7. Through him we have forgiveness for sins (Col 1:19-20): 'For in him all the fullness of God was pleased to dwell, and through him God was pleased to reconcile to himself all things, whether on earth or in heaven, by making peace through the blood of his cross.'

Great joy over little

Small things can give great happiness.
Such is the story of a Nazi prisoner:
The poor man was tortured every day.
One day they changed his cell.
In the new cell
there was a skylight,
through which he could see
a piece of blue sky
during the day
and a few stars
during the night.
The man was overjoyed
and wrote to his family
about this great fortune.
About his joy.
When I read this story,
I looked out my window.
I had all nature to appreciate.
I was free, not a prisoner,
I could go wherever I wanted!
And I think I felt the prayer of joy
of that poor prisoner.

41

God Is the Centre of All

1. Begin with a relaxation and silence exercise, such as no 6.
2. God is the centre of all. Now make a list of desires, as many as possible. Be sincere. In the sequence of values, where do God and seeking God fit? In the sequence of loves, where is love for the Father? Where is Jesus Christ found? Are there some desires that your conscience does not approve?
3. Consider carefully the means that exist for encouraging good desires and fleeing evil desires. Present each one of these means to God to be evaluated.
4. What is most important here are not the results, but being exposed and open to God; looking at each action, thought, and so forth coming from God and moving in that direction.
5. Do the same with your problems. Make a list and consider your problems one by one: How do you try to resolve this problem? Present these means to God. See what comes from God, what you feel as coming from the Spirit, who groans within you.

FOCUS

• This exercise purifies us for fully receiving God and God's gifts in our heart.
• All comes from God, and all must be offered in return.

CONTEMPLATION TO ATTAIN LOVE

God's Presence in His Gifts

1. God not only gives his gifts but is present in them (Acts 17:28): 'In him we live and move and have our being.'
2. God becomes present in the history of his people and with it he makes a covenant (Ex 33:7-11): 'And everyone who sought the Lord

would go out to the tent of meeting ... The Lord used to speak to Moses face to face, as one speaks to a friend.'

'I will put my law within them, and I will write it on their hearts; and I will be their God and they shall be my people' (Jer 31:33).

3. *In the excess of his love (Jn 1:14):* 'And the Word became flesh and lived among us.'

'... you will conceive in your womb and bear a son, and you will name him Jesus' (Lk 1:31). 'Look, the virgin shall conceive and bear a son. And they shall name him Emmanuel' (Mt 1:23).

4. *He dwelt among us (Jn 14:23):* 'Those who love me will keep my word, and my Father will love them, and we will come to them and make our home with them.'

5. *He is present sacramentally in the Eucharist (Jn 6:56):* 'Those who eat my flesh and drink my blood abide in me, and I in them.'

The Encounter

'How shall I encounter God?'
'Through desire,' answered the master.
One day they were both swimming in a river.
The master pushed the youth's head under water,
and the poor fellow
desperately sought to break free and to breathe.
The next day the master asked his disciple:
'Why did you struggle so hard
when I held your head under water?'
'Because I needed air.'
'Good – now when you feel the need for God
the way you felt the lack of air under water –
at that point,
you will know that you have encountered God!'

42

The Living Flame of Love

1. Begin with a relaxation and silence exercise, such as no 6.
2. The living flame of love. Calm yourself with a concentration exercise. Move into the centre of your being. Imagine flames of love pointing toward God, or fountains shooting upward.
3. Speak a word or phrase to give rhythm to this impulse. 'My God and my all!' 'Oh, Jesus!' 'Abba, Father!'
4. Listen to the word. Hear it grow and resonate everywhere in your being: head, heart ... until everything resounds with it.
5. Then feel that the word is invading the room, the house, and that it touches each person, the whole world. A cry, emerging from the depths of your being, emerges in your heart and expands throughout the world. That word is growing in your heart.

FOCUS

• This exercise is based in the 'darkness of the ignorance of the blind movement of love' of St John of the Cross.

CONTEMPLATION TO ATTAIN LOVE

God's Action in History

1. From the first page of the bible, God's action is present in history (Gen 1:1): 'In the beginning God created the heavens and the earth.' (Jn 1:1) 'See, I am making all things new' (Rev 21:5).
2. God's action is revealed in providence toward the chosen people with which he makes a covenant (Ex 33:19): 'Moses said, "Show me your glory, I pray." And he said, " ... and I will be their God, and they shall be my people"' (Jer 31:33).
3. But it is in Christ that God acts most evidently among human beings (Jn 1:3): 'All things came into being through him, and with-

out him not one thing came into being.' 'He is the image of the invisible God, the firstborn of all creation; for in him all things in heaven and on earth were created, things visible and invisible, whether thrones or dominions or rulers or powers – all things have been created through him and for him' (Col 1:15-16).

4. *In his name human beings are saved (1 Cor 6:11):* 'But you were washed, you were sanctified, you were justified in the name of the Lord Jesus Christ and in the Spirit of our God.'

5. *He prays for the unity of believers and brings it about (Jn 17:21):* '… that all may be one … so that the world may believe that you have sent me.' 'For he is our peace; in his flesh he has made both groups into one and has broken down the dividing wall, that is, the hostility between us' (Eph 2:14).

His action continues in the church

Go then,
make all peoples disciples,
baptising them in the name of the Father
and of the Son and of the Holy Spirit,
teaching them to observe
everything that I have commanded you.
And remember, I am with you always
to the end of time.
– *Mt 28:19-20*

43

The Name of Jesus in Creation

1. Begin with a relaxation and silence exercise, such as no 6.
2. The name of Jesus in creation. Christians hear this name throughout the entire creation. The whole world was created in Christ and through Christ.
3. Listen (in your imagination) to the waves of the sea, the sounds of a river, the breeze in the trees, the music of the stars moving across the firmament, the silence of the night, everything glorifies this name.
4. Listen to the name of Jesus in the rhythm of mechanical sounds: motors, machines, cars.
5. Listen to the name of Jesus in the rhythm of instrumental or choral music.
6. Listen to the name of Jesus resounding in your heart!
7. Listen to the entire universe shouting for you and see it moving toward you. The Spirit and the bride say 'Come!' 'If these [the disciples] were silent, the stones would cry out' (Lk 19:40).

FOCUS

• The grace of this prayer is to confer on us the vision of Christian wisdom that enables us to view everything under the gaze, in the light, of the Word Incarnate out of Love. Thus for us Christ is Light, Christ is a fountain of living water, the fountain of all that is good and all grace for us.

• The world, events, and people are transfigured by the light of Christ, and they can be be understood only through this light. The movement thereby becomes complete: from things to God, who is present in them and acting for our good, and from God, the source of all good, the highest goodness, Christ the Saviour, image of the Father, we descend to what is most interior to, and deepest in, creatures. From created things to the Creator! From the Creator to created things!

CONTEMPLATION TO ATTAIN LOVE

All Good Things Come from On High

1. *Everything comes from on high, beginning with Jesus Christ (Jn:1:14):* 'And the Word became flesh and lived among us, and we have seen his glory, the glory as of a father's only son, full of grace and truth.'

'From his fullness we have all received grace for grace. The law indeed was given through Moses; grace and truth came through Jesus Christ' (Jn 1:16).

2. *Seeing everything in Christ (Cor 1:15-20):* 'He is the image of the invisible God, the firstborn of all creation; for in him all things in heaven and on earth were created, things visible and invisible, whether thrones or dominions or rulers or powers – all things have been created through him and for him. He himself is before all things, and in him all things hold together. He is the head of the body the church; he is the beginning, the firstborn from the dead, so that he might come to have the first place in everything. For in him all the fullness of God was pleased to dwell, and through him God was pleased to reconcile to himself all things, whether on earth or in heaven, by making peace through the blood of his cross.'

3. *Christ is the fountain (Jn 7:37-38):*

'On the last day of the festival, the great day, while Jesus was standing there, he cried out, Let anyone who is thirsty come to me, and let the one who believes in me drink. As the scripture has said, out of the believer's heart shall flow rivers of living water.'

'But those who drink of the water that I will give them will never be thirsty. The water that I will give will become in them a spring of water gushing up to eternal life' (Jn 4:14).

4. *Christ is the light (Jn 1:8):* John 'himself was not the Light, but he came to testify to the light.'

'I am the light of the world. Whoever follows me will never walk in darkness, but will have the light of life' (Jn 8:12).

5. Everything works together for good (Rom 8:28):
'We know that all things work together for good for those who love God, who are called according to his purpose.'

Suggested Readings

de Mello, Anthony, *Sadhana: A Way to God: Christian Exercises in Eastern Form*, Series IV, Study Aids in Jesuit Topics, no. 9 (St Louis: Institute of Jesuit Sources, 1978).

_____, *The Song of the Bird* (Garden City, N.Y.: Image Books, 1984).

_____, *One Minute Wisdom* (Garden City, N.Y.: Doubleday, 1986).

_____, *The Heart of the Enlightened: A Book of Story Meditations* (New York: Doubleday, 1989).

_____, *Awareness: A de Mello Spirituality Conference in His Own Words* (New York: Doubleday, 1990).

_____, *Contact with God: Retreat Conferences* (Anand, India: Gujarat Sahitya Prakash, 1990).

_____, *One Minute Nonsense* (Chicago: Loyola University Press, 1992).

_____, *The way to Love: The Last Meditations of Anthony de Mello* (New York: Doubleday, 1992).

_____, *More One Minute Nonsense* (Chicago: Loyola University Press, 1993).

Galache, Gabriel, C. *Guia Interior*, 2nd. ed (Sao Paulo: Edições Loyola, 1995).

_____, *Jesus Bate à Nossa Porta*, 2nd ed (Sao Paulo: Edições Loyola, 1995).

_____, *Das Criaturas ao Criador* (Sao Paulo: Edições Loyola, 1995).

Paul VI, *Populorum Progressio* (PP).

Loyola, St Ignatius, *The Spiritual Exercises of St Ignatius*,

Translated by Anthony Mottola (New York: Doubleday-Image, 1964).

Valesa, Father, *Mastering Sadhana: On Retreat with Anthony de Mello* (New York: Image Books, 1988).

Vatican II, *Gaudium et Spes* (GS).